STUDIES IN HISTORY, ECONOMICS
AND PUBLIC LAW

Edited by the
FACULTY OF POLITICAL SCIENCE OF
COLUMBIA UNIVERSITY

NUMBER 446

LABOR LEGISLATION IN CZECHOSLOVAKIA

With Special Reference to the Standards of the International Labor Organization

BY

ESTHER BLOSS

LABOR LEGISLATION IN CZECHOSLOVAKIA

With Special Reference to the Standards of the International Labor Organization

BY

ESTHER BLOSS, Ph. D.

NEW YORK
COLUMBIA UNIVERSITY PRESS
LONDON: P. S. KING & SON, LTD.
1938

PRINTED IN THE UNITED STATES OF AMERICA

ACKNOWLEDGMENT

The author wishes to express her gratitude and thanks to Professor Samuel McCune Lindsay for his guidance in the preparation of this work. Without his advice, encouragement, and assistance, its completion would have been impossible.

The author is indebted to Mr. Josef Hanč, Czechoslovak Consul in New York, for his courteous attention and generous help in securing from Prague materials which would otherwise have been inaccessible to her.

She is also greatly indebted and very thankful to Mr. Harold B. Butler, Director of the International Labor Office, Geneva, and to various members of several technical services of the Office for their interest in her study, and for many valuable materials and suggestions contributed by them. However, she alone is responsible for any errors of fact, misinterpretations, or other shortcomings in the completed work. She cannot hope to have added anything to the wealth of knowledge on this subject to be found in the International Labor Office. But she does hope that her efforts may stimulate others to use the materials available in Geneva for a continuation of this study of Czechoslovak legislation and for similar studies of legislation in other countries in order to bring about a better understanding of the great pioneer work which the I. L. O. is doing.

TABLE OF CONTENTS

PAGE

CHAPTER III

Special Provisions for the Protection of Women

PART II

Social Insurance

CHAPTER IV

Sickness Insurance

CHAPTER V

Old-Age and Invalidity, Widows' and Orphans' Insurance and Pensions

PAGE

CHAPTER VI

(1) Workmen's Compensation

(2) Use of White Lead, Phosphorus, and Other Poisonous Substances

CHAPTER VII

Unemployment Insurance

PAGE

PART III

Other Aspects of Labor Legislation; Summary and Conclusion

CHAPTER VIII

(1) Participation of Workers in Management

(2) Emigration

(3) Holidays With Pay

CHAPTER IX

Czechoslovakia and the International Labor Organization

INTRODUCTION

THE independent state of Czechoslovakia came into existence officially by virtue of Section VII of the Treaty of Peace between the Allied and Associated Powers and Germany, signed at Versailles on June 28, 1919. In this treaty Germany agreed that the Czechoslovak State should include the autonomous territory of the Ruthenians to the south of the Carpathians, and ceded a part of Prussian Silesia inhabited by Czechs, to the new state.[1]

The Treaty of Peace with Austria, signed at St. Germain on Sept. 10, 1919,[2] recognized the complete independence of the Czechoslovak State, and renounced "all rights and title over the territories of the former Austro-Hungarian Monarchy situated outside the frontiers of Austria, as laid down by Part II, Article 27, and recognized in accordance with the present treaty as forming part of the Czechoslovak State", which included the provinces of Bohemia, Moravia, and Silesia.

On the same day, September 10, 1919, at St. Germain, a treaty was signed by the principal allied and associated powers and Czechoslovakia,[3] by which the United States, Great Britain, France, Italy, and Japan confirmed their recognition of the Czechoslovak State "as a sovereign and independent member of the Family of Nations within the boundaries determined in accordance with the terms of the Treaty of Peace with Austria", and Czechoslovakia on the other hand, undertook to "assume full and complete protection of life and liberty to all inhabitants of Czechoslovakia without distinction of birth, nationality, language, race, or religion."

Lastly, the Treaty with Hungary,[4] signed at Trianon on June 4, 1920, recognized the independence of Czechoslovakia, fixed the frontier between Hungary and Czechoslovakia, and provided that Hungary cede to the new state Slovakia and part of Ruthenia.

Czechoslovakia, thus set up by the treaties with Germany, Austria, and Hungary, in 1919-20, has an area of approximately 54,000 square miles. In size, it ranks fourteenth among the European nations. The area is divided as follows: Bohemia 20,097; Moravia 8,611; Silesia 1,707; Slovakia 18,924; and Ruthenia 4,901 square miles. In addition to the Czechoslovaks, constituting two-thirds of 15,000,000 inhabitants of Czechoslovakia according to the census of 1930, the other third is made up of 3,300,000 Germans, 700,000 Magyars, 550,000 Ruthenians (two-thirds of which are Russians) and the remainder (450,000) Poles and Jews, the latter constituting a large minority in the cities. The population, however, is not evenly distributed, the territories of Silesia, Bohemia, and Moravia being more densely populated than Slovakia or Ruthenia. The mountainous districts of central and eastern Slovakia and the mountainous northern part of Ruthenia are the least populous.

In regard to the occupations of the people, agriculture and industry are about equally represented. In Slovakia and Ruthenia, agriculture is the main occupation, whereas in Bohemia, Moravia, and Silesia, the majority of the people are engaged in manufacturing and mining. The greater part of the industries of the former Austro-Hungarian Empire are in the three last named provinces. The industries taken over by Czechoslovakia include 92 per cent of the sugar factories, 65 per cent of the breweries, 95 per cent of the malt factories, 50 per cent of the liquor industry, 90 per cent of the glass industry, 70 per cent of the leather industry, and the greater part of the textile industry. Czechoslovakia also took over about 75 per cent of the Austro-Hungarian chemical industry, 70 per cent of the paper industry, and 80 per cent of the building and ceramic industries. In regard to mining, the three territories of Bohemia, Moravia, and Silesia contain 79 per cent of the coal mines of Austria-Hungary, and in 1915 produced 85 per cent of the total output of coal of the Empire.[5] All these industrial concerns which came under the jurisdiction of the new Czechoslovak State were operated previously under Austro-Hungarian industrial and labor law.

The independence of Czechoslovakia was proclaimed in Paris on October 18, 1918, by the Czechoslovak National Council under the leadership of Masaryk, Beneš, and Stefanik. This proclamation, the first constitutional law of free Czechoslovakia, was a liberal document. It rejected the divine right of kings for " the principles of Lincoln and of the Declaration of the Rights of Man." It went on to declare that " our democracy shall rest on universal suffrage; women shall be placed on an equal footing with men politically, socially, and culturally, while the right of the minority shall be safeguarded by proportional representation. . . . The Czechoslovak Nation will carry out far-reaching social and economic reforms. . . . On the basis of democracy, mankind will be reorganized. . . . We believe in democracy, we believe in liberty, and liberty for evermore." [6]

The permanent constitution,[7] promulgated February 29, 1920, declared that " the Czechoslovak state shall be a Democratic Republic " and that " the territories of the Czechoslovak Republic shall form a united and indivisible unit. . . ." The legislative power of the whole Czechoslovak Republic is vested in a Parliament composed of two houses. The Chamber of Deputies is made up of three hundred members who must be Czechoslovak citizens thirty years of age or over, elected for a term of six years by all citizens of the Czechoslovak Republic who are at least twenty-one years of age. The Senate consists of one hundred and fifty members who must be Czechoslovak citizens forty-five years of age or over, elected for a term of eight years by all citizens of the Czechoslovak Republic who are at least twenty-six years of age. Members of both houses are " elected according to a general, equal, direct, and secret suffrage on a basis of proportional representation."

Proposals for legislation may originate either with the Government or in either chamber. Laws are valid only with the consent of both chambers, except " that a measure passed by the Chamber of Deputies becomes a law in spite of an adverse decision of the Senate, if the Chamber of Deputies declares by a majority of 50 per cent of all its members that it adheres to its first decision." Should Parliament reject a bill presented by the Government, the latter can by unanimous consent, proclaim a referendum in which all citizens may vote who are qualified to vote for the Chamber of Deputies.

Both houses, meeting in joint session, elect the president of the Republic who may be any citizen of the Czechoslovak Republic eligible to the Chamber of Deputies who is not less than thirty-five years of age. His term is seven years. He has the right "to return with comment any law enacted by Parliament. Should both chambers, by ballot, taken on roll call, affirm the returned bill by a majority of 50 per cent of all their members, the bill shall become law. Should the bill not receive a majority of votes in both chambers, the bill becomes law, provided that the Chamber of Deputies in the new ballot, taken by roll call, passes it by a three-fifths majority of all its members." The President also has the power to convoke and dissolve Parliament, and to appoint and dismiss Cabinet ministers.

The Government, composed of the Prime Minister and other ministers, is responsible to the Chamber of Deputies, which may vote a lack of confidence in it. Such a vote is valid "if more than half of all the members are present, if a 50 per cent majority be obtained, and if the vote be taken by roll call." In case of a vote of lack of confidence, the Government resigns to the President who then determines who shall direct governmental affairs until a new Government is formed. Every Government decree must be signed by the Prime Minister and the minister invested with its execution.

Section V of the Constitution deals with the rights, liberties, and duties of citizens. It declares that no privileges due to sex, birth, or occupation shall be recognized, and that all persons residing in the Czechoslovak Republic shall enjoy equally with the citizens of the Republic, complete security of life and liberty "without regard to origin, nationality, language, race, or religion." Every person may "within the limits of the law" express his opinion orally or in writing. The right to assemble peaceably and to form associations is guaranteed. "The right of petition shall be enjoyed by every person."

Section VI provides for the protection of national, religious, and racial minorities. It states that "all citizens of the Czechoslovak Republic shall be in all respects equal before the law and shall enjoy equal civic and political rights whatever be their race, their language, or their religion."

The Constitution was accompanied by an Enabling Act of the same date, containing the necessary provisions for putting it into force, and carrying on the Government in the interim. The important feature of the Enabling Act is its thoroughgoing insistence upon the supremacy of the Constitution and the laws in conformity with it. The power of holding laws unconstitutional is vested by the Enabling Act in a Constitutional Court composed of two members chosen by the Supreme Court, two chosen by the Supreme Administrative Court, and three including the President, named by the President of the Republic.

The people of Czechoslovakia, particularly those who lived in the highly industrialized provinces of Bohemia, Moravia, and Silesia, had had under Austrian rule a considerable, if none too favorable, experience with labor legislation. In Austria, the beginnings of labor legislation and its administration may be traced back to the end of the eighteenth century.

Chancellor's decrees of 1786 and 1787 regulated the work of factory apprentices. A compulsory school attendance law was passed in 1805. Little was done from then until 1842 when the first important attempt was made to protect workers in factories. The Decree of June 11, 1842, limited the work of children under twelve years, but permitted children over nine to work if they had had three years' schooling. The hours of work were limited to ten for children from nine to twelve, and twelve for those over twelve years of age. Night work between 9 P.M. and 5 A.M. was prohibited. One hour midday pause was allowed.

In 1854 the first law for the protection of workers in mines was passed and on December 20, 1859, the first Industrial Code relating to establishments employing more than twenty persons was decreed. Child labor was prohibited before ten years of age. The work of children between ten and fourteen was limited to ten hours, and of those between fourteen and sixteen to twelve hours. The new Industrial Code of 1885 was the basis of the labor legislation existing in Austria at the outbreak of the World War.

The laws for the protection of workers were not properly administered or enforced until the institution of factory inspection in 1883. The enforcement of the law of 1842 was given to the local authorities consisting of the administrative police, district school superintendents, and local clergymen. It was generally admitted that the laws from 1842 to 1883 were dead letters. Exploitation of workers by their employers continued, child labor was common, and there was little attempt at the enforcement of the provisions of the various acts.[8]

At the outbreak of the World War in 1914, the Industrial Code of Austria was based on the text issued by the Ministers of Commerce and Interior on August 16, 1907, and consisted of a consolidation of various previous acts, as follows: December 20, 1859; March 15, 1883; March 8, 1885; June 16, 1895; November 27, 1896; February 23, 1897; February 25, 1902; July 22, 1902; July 18, 1905; and February 5, 1907. Besides these laws, there are a number of decrees and orders included in the second part of the Industrial Code.

The Code is divided into ten chapters of which the most important is the sixth, which deals with protection of industrial employees, as follows:

The provisions regulating hours of employment, the limitation of work, and other conditions for the work of women and children are contained in articles 93, 94, 95, and 96 of this chapter. Article 94 consists of the following provsions:

1. The prohibition of children from working before the completion of 12 years of age.

2. Young persons between 12 and 14 years of age may work in industries if their health is not injured by the work, and it does not prevent their bodily development or interfere with the legal school requirements.

3. The duration of work of these young employees must not exceed eight hours.

The ministers of commerce and interior may interpret and amplify these provisions, also designate those industries in which young persons and women may not work at all or only under certain conditions.

4. Women must not be allowed to work within four weeks after parturition.

Article 95 deals with night work, prohibiting the regular industrial employment of young persons under 16 years of age between the hours of 8 p. m. and 5 a. m.

Article 96 deals with:

1. The keeping of certain registers for young employees.

2. The limitation of the daily hours of labor of all employees in factory establishments to not more than 11 hours within 24 hours.

The ministers are allowed to make exceptions to this rule in case of need. Overtime is to be properly remunerated. A section of this article, designated as 96b, provides also that:

1. Children may not be employed regularly in factory establishments before reaching 14 years of age.

2. Young persons between 14 and 16 years of age may be employed only at light work which is not injurious to health, or does not interfere with their physical development.

3. Women are included in the same provisions as young persons as far as their exclusion from night work in factory plants is concerned.

The provisions for prevention of accidents, regulation of dangerous trades, and all sanitary regulations in factories and workshops are based upon article 74 in Chapter 6. This article reads as follows:

1. Every employer shall be obligated to provide and maintain at his own expense such sanitary arrangements and other appliances as the nature of the industry or working place requires for the protection of the lives and health of the employees.

2. Industrial employers must in particular see to it that machines, appliances, and their parts are so fenced in or protected that workmen, so long as they observe the required precautions in performing their work, are not easily liable to injury.

3. It is also the duty of industrial employers to see that during working hours the workrooms shall be kept as well lighted, clean, and free from dust as possible, according to the nature of the industry, and that if necessary the work rooms shall be sufficiently illuminated by artificial light, and that they shall be ventilated according to the number of workers and illuminating appliances and counteracting all possible influence of injurious gases, and further that operation shall be so arranged that the health of the employees is protected as much as possible.

4. Industrial employers who furnish housing accommodations to their employees must take care that only such rooms are used for this purpose as are not likely to injure the physical safety, health, and morals of the employees, and in which a sufficient quantity of pure water for drinking and other purposes is available, as far as local conditions permit.

5. Finally, employers who employ women and girls and young persons under 18 years of age are obligated to properly safeguard their morals, as required by age and sex.[9]

Factory inspection was based upon the Law of June 17, 1883 and subsequent laws, as well as upon ministerial orders, rules, and regulations issued after that date. All industrial establishments, except mines and quarries, were under the supervision of industrial inspectors. The duties of the industrial inspectors are defined by Article 5 of the Law of June 17, 1883, as follows:

The supervision of the enforcement of the provisions of the Industrial Code:

1. As to measures to be taken and appliances to be provided by the employer to protect the lives and health of the workers in the workrooms as well as in dwellings provided by the employer (upon this provision are based the various ministerial decrees and orders as to prevention of accidents and sanitary regulations of industrial establishments);

2. As to the employment of workers, daily hours of labor, and periodical rest periods;

3. As to the keeping of registers, posting of shop rules, wage payments, and workmen's pass books; and

4. As to the technical instruction of juvenile workers.[10]

The Ministry of Commerce was the administrative body which enforced the Industrial Code. It appointed inspectors, interpreted the Industrial Code, received reports from the central inspector, determined the inspection districts, designated the inspectors for each district, and had full control of the industrial inspection service.

This constitutes a very brief outline of the labor legislation in Austria up to 1914. A more detailed account of Austrian legislation and several references to Hungarian legislation prior to 1914 will be found infra under specific topics, to show how the new laws of Czechoslovakia grew out of the early legislation of the Dual Monarchy.

When the Czech people with their long experience under the labor legislation of Austria became independent, they were in a position, under the terms of their democratic Constitution, to pass further measures of labor legislation which they had long desired, but had not been able to realize under Austrian rule. Under the guidance of a Minister of Social Welfare in their Cabinet, and with the cooperation of their numerous political parties and labor organizations, the parliament representing the Czech people has, in the past twenty years, passed such a volume of labor legislation as to put Czechoslovakia in the first rank of modern progressive countries. The standards set up by the Czechoslovak labor legislation in many cases parallel and in some instances surpass those of the International Labor Conventions.

It was this fact which influenced me to undertake this study of the labor legislation of Czechoslovakia. Having studied for some time the work of the International Labor Organization with increasing interest in its aims, I determined to find out whether its Conventions were ideals only, or how far they found realization in the legislation of the European countries. It was my first intention to study the labor laws of several of the smaller European countries, possibly Czechoslovakia, Poland, and Belgium, and to see how their legislation compared with the standards of the I.L.O. Conventions. Starting with Czechoslovakia, I became so much interested in the remarkable record of that country in the few years since it became independent, that I decided to confine my study to the labor legislation of Czechoslovakia.

The author has been able to use only the materials available in English, French, and German, and only a few documentary sources in the Czech language through English, French, and German translations. The comprehensive materials and records to be found in the publications of the I.L.O. have been exhaustively studied. Particularly valuable for this study have been the Proceedings of the International Labor Conferences, the Annual Reports of the Director, the Summary of Reports at each Conference under Article 22 (Article 408, old number for Annual Reports to the 19th Session, 1935 inclusive), the supplementary reports of the Committee of Experts on the Application of Conventions, and the Minutes of the Governing Body; the Minutes of the Committee on Enforcement of Conventions (Article 408 or Article 22), the Annual Review, 1930, and the Yearbooks 1931 to 1936-37, the Yearbooks of Labor Statistics for the years issued; the complete files of the International Labor Review (Monthly, Vol. I, 1921, to Vol. XXXVI, 1937); Industrial and Labor Information (Weekly

Vol. I, 1922, to Vol. LXIV, 1937). The Studies and Reports to date were examined in search of record material pertinent to the subject in hand.

The methods employed have been those of a descriptive and analytical study, with some attempt at critical comment and evaluation. The materials available within the limitations indicated were not sufficient to warrant a theoretical study of their implications or of the underlying principles of international minimum labor standards or the possibilities of their extension.

The author feels, however, that the results of this study, by concentrating upon a single country, may stimulate others to undertake objective studies of particular areas and the development of labor legislation therein, in relation to the standards of the I.L.O. This method of approach may be one way of measuring more concretely the indirect results as well as the direct effect of the activities of the I.L.O.

---

1 Senate Document No. 49, 66th Congress, 1st Session (Washington: Government Printing Office, 1919), p. 44.

2 Treaty of Peace between the Allied and Associated Powers and Austria, together with other Treaties, Agreements, etc., signed at Saint-Germain-en-Laye, Sept. 10, 1919 (London: His Majesty's Stationery Office, 1921), p. 44.

3 *Op. cit.*, p. 181.

4 Treaty of Peace between the Allied and Associated Powers and Hungary, *International Law Documents* (Washington: Government Printing Office, 1920), p. 199.

5 Josef Gruber, Editor, *Czechoslovakia, A Survey of Economic and Social Conditions* (N. Y.: Macmillan Co., 1924), pp. 1-11; *Encyclopaedia Britannica*, 14th ed.; VI, 952; W. C. Langsam, *The World Since 1914* (N. Y.: Macmillan, 1936), pp. 552-565.

6 *Declaration of Independence of the Czechoslovak Nation* by its Provisional Government, Oct. 18, 1918 (N. Y.: Marchbanks Press, 1918).

7 McBain and Rogers, *New Constitutions of Europe* (Garden City, N. Y.: Doubleday, Page & Co., 1923), p. 310.

8 G. M. Price, *Administration of Labor Laws* (U. S. Dept. of Labor, Bureau of Labor Statistics, Bulletin # 142, Washington: Government Printing Office, 1914), p. 214.

9 Price, *op. cit.*, p. 215.

10 Price, *op. cit.*, p. 218.

PART I

CONDITIONS OF WORK

CHAPTER I

GENERAL PROVISIONS FOR THE PROTECTION OF WORKERS

A. In Austria Prior to 1918

1. SCOPE

Austrian labor legislation before the War consisted of two sets of fairly distinct measures: those which regulated industrial labor generally, and those which concerned labor in mines. The nucleus of the first group of measures is the Industrial Code of 1885. The provisions of the Code and subsequent acts which amended and supplemented it applied to factories and to commercial establishments, i. e., shops and stores. They did not apply to agriculture or forestry or to the industrial occupations connected therewith; nor did they apply to unskilled manual labor, to domestic service, to industrial occupations carried on by the members of the employer's family, to transportatoin by rail or ship, to navigation by sea, canals, or rivers, nor to sea fishing.

2. MAXIMUM WORKDAY AND REST PERIODS

The maximum duration of the workday in factories was eleven hours in twenty-four, not counting intervals of rest. In all industrial establishments there must be intervals of rest amounting to one and one-half hours. This total period of rest included at least one full hour at midday unless the nature of the industry did not permit it. The Minister of Commerce might, after consultation with the Minister of the Interior and the Chambers of Commerce and Industry, permit a modification of the rules concerning intervals of rest in certain industries in which the interruption of work was impracticable. He might also determine the industries in which, upon proof of necessity, the maximum workday in factories might be raised from eleven to twelve hours. This list must be revised every three years. After the same preliminaries, the Minister of Commerce might designate the industries in which continuous operation was permitted by means of shifts of labor.

Whenever work was stopped by forces beyond human control, or by accident, or whenever it was necessary to increase the output, the authorities in charge of the enforcement of the industrial laws might permit a temporary prolongation of the workday for a total period of not more than three weeks. The right to grant this privilege for a longer period belonged to the provincial administration. In cases of urgent necessity, the workday might be prolonged for a period of not more than three days in any one month, by notifying the local authorities in charge of the enforcement of the industrial laws. These provisions limiting the duration of the workday did not apply to auxiliary tasks that formed no part of the industrial process, such as getting up steam, cleaning, etc.

The right to work twelve hours a day instead of eleven was granted to a considerable number of industries by the Ordinance of May 27, 1885, but was later withdrawn from a number of the most important ones, such as wool and cotton spinning. Frequent abuses of the right to work overtime led to the passage of the Ordinance of December 12, 1895, which provided that permission to prolong the workday beyond eleven hours should not be granted for a longer period than fifteen weeks in any year, nor to the owners of establishments not fulfilling the requirements of hygiene, nor to employers who employed their laborers overtime without first obtaining the required authorization.

On January 14, 1910, a law was passed regulating the hours of rest in mercantile establishments, shops, stores, and concerns for the carrying and forwarding of goods. It provided that laborers in these occupations must have eleven hours of rest out of twenty-four. An exception was made for wagon drivers, for whom the minimum was ten hours. The midday rest period must, as a rule, amount to one and one-half hours. Shops for the sale of goods, and offices connected therewith, must close from 8 P.M. to 5 A.M. Those shops selling food products, however, might remain open until 9 P.M. The rest periods might be shortened on not more than thirty days in the year in the following cases: when inventories were made; when a concern was started or moved; and when work was imperative to keep goods from spoiling. These rules could be set aside entirely at health resorts during the "season".

For all laborers in mines, the maximum workday according to the Law of June 21, 1884, was twelve hours including pauses for rest and also including the time for descent and ascent. The law specified ten hours of actual work in the mine. Exceptions might be granted by the Minister of Agriculture in favor of mines at high altitude in the Alpine region, but the total number of hours must not exceed sixty per week. The administrative officials having supervision of mines might in cases of necessity, grant a prolongation of the maximum workday.

The Law of June 27, 1901, concerning coal mines, provided that laborers employed in mining the coal must not be employed more than nine hours a day including pauses. This limitation, however, did not apply to mines in which the working period was longer than nine hours at the time the law went into effect. For such mines, the usual limit of twelve hours, or ten hours of actual work remained in force. According to this law also, the Minister of Agriculture might grant exceptions for coal mines at high altitudes, though the total number of hours' work therein must not exceed fifty-four per week. The mining officials might extend the maximum limit up to twelve hours a day in case of temporary necessity.

3. SUNDAY REST

It was provided by the Code of 1885 (modified by the laws of 1895 and 1905) that industrial labor should, as a rule, cease on Sunday. It stated that Sunday rest must begin not later than 6 A.M., must last twenty-four hours, and must be simultaneous for all laborers in each establishment. The following exceptions were provided:

a. The provisions concerning Sunday rest did not apply to the labor of the employer himself if done privately and without aid of employees.

b. They did not apply to work that could not be postponed, or to the work of cleaning and repairing that could not be carried on at other times without danger to employees or without serious interference with the business of the establishment.

c. They did not apply to the work of watchmen and caretakers of industrial establishments.

d. They did not apply to temporary work that could not be postponed and that was required by public interest, public safety, or circumstances of necessity.

e. For the purpose of taking an inventory, the Sunday regulations might be suspended once a year.

f. In mercantile establishments, Sunday work was permitted for a period of not longer than four hours. On certain Sundays during periods of exceptional activity (like Christmas) work might be allowed for eight hours.

g. In certain occupations in which an interruption of activity was impracticable or in which the needs of the public made work on Sunday necessary, public ordinances might permit Sunday work. In this connection, administrative ordinances enumerated over fifty industries or occupations in which employees might work on Sundays under certain stipulated conditions.

The legislation regarding Sunday rest was in a chaotic condition, for in the thirteen administrative subdivisions of the Empire, fifty-eight local ordinances on the subject were passed between 1905 and 1909. By these ordinances, approximately a thousand different régimes were established for different occupations and localities.

4. HYGIENE AND SAFETY

Every employer was obliged, at his own expense, to provide such safety appliances and to adopt such measures as might be necessary to protect the life, limb, and health of his employees against dangers arising from the occupation in which they were employed. The workplaces must be kept clean and as free from dust as the nature of the industry permitted. If an employer furnished lodging for his laborers, the rooms must not be unhealthful.[1]

B. In Hungary Prior to 1918

Very little had been done in Hungary in the way of labor legislation up to 1918. According to the *Handwörterbuch der Staatswissenschaften*, labor legislation in Hungary was " noch in statu nascenti ". Practically the only labor or industrial law, aside from those laws passed for the special protection of women and children which will be found infra under those topics, was a law passed in 1891 [2] providing that industrial work must cease on Sunday and on St. Stephen's Day. In this law, exceptions were made in the case of work necessary for cleaning and putting premises in order. The law empowered the Minister of Commerce to decide what classes of industry needed continuous work. In such industries, work might be continued even on holidays. But in these cases, Sunday rest must be granted to workmen alternately.

C. In Czechoslovakia

1. SCOPE

The first of the labor laws of the new Czechoslovak Republic, both in point of time and in importance, was the Act respecting the Eight Hour Working Day [3] which was passed by the National Assembly under the Provisional Government on December 19, 1918, and went into force on January 3, 1919. It applies to undertakings, works, and institutions carried on by the State, and by public or private associations, funds, societies, and companies of a profit-making, public utility, or charitable nature. It also applies to mining, and to agriculture and forestry with respect to employees who live outside the household of the employer and who are regularly employed for daily, weekly, or monthly wages. A circular issued by the Minister of Social Welfare on March 21, 1919,[4] explains the scope of the Act more fully. It states that the Eight Hour Act regulates the labor of all workers. Therefore it applies not only to workmen in the narrow sense, but to both manual and professional workers, regardless of status.

The Act applies to persons engaged in industry and commerce, and also to persons employed in the law courts and by notaries, stockbrokers, civil engineers, and agencies; to those employed in doctors' consulting rooms, in hospitals, in banks and insurance offices, in public places of entertainment, and in the production of periodical publications; to employees of productive and distributive cooperative societies; to commercial travellers, firemen, school attendants, etc.

The Circular states that in agriculture and forestry, all persons come under the Act who are in regular employment and who do not live in their employer's house. The Act also regulates the hours of work of persons engaged in household duties, unless they have been employed for temporary work lasting less than six days. The Act does not apply to home work unless it is in continuation of work done at a work place. The employer is forbidden to give out work to persons employed in his undertaking to be done at home in order to lengthen the hours of work. This procedure is permissible only when the employer has previously obtained a permit for overtime.

2. MAXIMUM WORKDAY, BREAKS, AND SUNDAY REST

The Act Respecting the Eight Hour Working Day states that the actual hours of work may not exceed eight hours per day or forty-eight hours per week. The distribution of the daily and weekly hours of work and the fixing of definite breaks in work is left to agreements between employers and workers. However, at least a quarter of an hour's break must be allowed after not more than five hours' uninterrupted work. The worker must be allowed an uninterrupted period of rest of at least thirty-two hours in every week. In undertakings in which the processes can be interrupted without difficulty, this period of rest must as a rule fall on Sundays.

In the Order of January 11, 1919,[5] issued by the Minister of Social Welfare to supplement the Eight Hour Day Act, certain groups of undertakings are allowed to distribute their hours of work over four weeks in any way desired, provided that within this period the total number of hours does not exceed 192. These undertakings are: agricultural undertakings, horticulture, tile works, glass works, pottery works, foundries, mills driven by water, breweries, building operations, manufacture of soda water, waterworks, work connected with the procuring of natural ice, forwarding and transport undertakings, river and sun baths, electricity works, and lumbering.

Also in this Order, permission was granted to certain continuous process undertakings to extend the daily or weekly hours for the purpose of alternating shifts, on condition that the workers have their thirty-two hours' weekly rest on a Sunday at least every third week, and that the hours by which the weekly total of forty-eight is exceeded when the shifts are alternated are paid for as overtime. These undertakings are: iron works, metal works, enamelling works, lime kilns, brick works, kaolin washing works, pottery works, glass works, works for the manufacture of carbon electrodes, works for the manufacture of accumulators, of goods from wood fibre, of cork sheets, of cellulose, water mills, maltworks, works for the drying and sulphuring of hops, sugar factories, liquorice works, syrup and grape sugar works, drying works for chicory, beets, potatoes, and fruits, jam, fruit pulp, and sausage factories, spirit distilleries, starch works, chemical works, fat works, petroleum refineries, works for the manufacture of gas for light, heat, and power, and independent electrical works.

a. *Recent Reduction of Hours of Work*

During recent years the Government has taken various steps for the purpose of reducing hours below the limits fixed by law. Ministerial decisions were issued in 1933 and 1934, introducing the forty-hour week in public works and works carried on with the assistance of Government grants.[6] As regards private industry, agreements have been concluded, particularly in 1935, under Government auspices, providing for a forty or forty-two hour week in the glass bottle, shoe, yeast, artificial silk, brewery, alcohol, and other industries.[7]

3. OVERTIME

When extra work is necessary in case of an interruption of the undertaking resulting from "force majeure" or accident, or in the public interest, particular undertakings may be permitted to increase the hours of work during not more than four weeks of the year, and by not more than two hours per day. These permits are issued for works subject to industrial inspection, by the industrial inspector; for mining undertakings, by the district mining board; for railway work, by the Minister of Railways; for undertakings and institutions in agriculture and forestry, by the communal authorities; and for other undertakings, works, and institutions, by the political authorities of first instance. Also, overtime not exceeding two hours per day during not more than sixteen weeks in the year may be granted under the same circumstances for mining undertakings, for railway work, for agriculture and forestry, and for other works and undertakings. All of these extra hours of work count as overtime and are especially remunerated.

Overtime must not extend beyond twenty weeks or two hundred and forty hours per year. This limitation, however, does not apply to emergency work, especially repairs, where danger to life, health, and the public interest is involved. For emergency work of this kind which cannot be carried out within the usual hours of work, no official permission is necessary. Nor is special permission necessary for subsidiary operations which necessarily precede or follow the work, such as the heating of boilers, cleaning workrooms, and feeding animals, even when such undertakings are carried on outside the ordinary hours of work.

If longer working hours are temporarily necessary in other occupations besides those enumerated in the Order of January 11, 1919, that is in hotels and public houses, in the production of goods for the Christmas market, in making balance sheets, and in stock taking, this need can be met by the issue of permits for overtime.

a. *Collective Agreements*

In Section 6 (3) and (4) of the Eight Hour Day Law, certain questions are left to be dealt with by way of collective agreements: e. g. the calculation of average hours of work and the rate of remuneration for overtime. In many cases the collective agreements also fix a limit in respect of hours of work lower than that laid down by legislation.[8]

The Legislative Decree of June 15, 1934 (the validity of which was prolonged until the end of 1938) provided for the compulsory prolongation of the validity of collective agreements (unless a new agreement was concluded),[9] and this has been a factor in the stabilization of wages during the recent crisis, preventing them from falling too low, but, when recovery took place, preventing wages from rising too rapidly.

The Legislative Decree of April 29, 1935 (the validity of which was subsequently prolonged until the end of 1940) regulated the application of collective agreements in the textile industry. Under this decree, a collective agreement may be declared compulsory in a specified district for all textile undertakings belonging to a certain branch of the industry, wherever such agreement regulates the conditions of work of not less than 70 per cent of the workers employed in the undertakings belonging to that branch in the district concerned. A collective agreement may further be extended to cover undertakings in a neighboring district.[10]

The Legislative Decree of June 26, 1937 made it possible to apply a similar procedure to all industries in general.[11]

4. NIGHT WORK

Night work, that is, work during the hours between 10 P.M. and 5 A.M., is allowed only in continuous industries in which the manufacturing process cannot be interrupted for technical reasons. In other undertakings, it is permissible only when it is necessary in the public interest or in order to satisfy a regular public need. Temporary night work, due to the necessity of repairs, is permissible if the regular progress of the undertaking would otherwise be endangered for a considerable period.

5. HOME WORK

Attempts to regulate the working hours in home industries were made in Austria but without any practical results. The Law of December 12, 1919,[12] regulating working conditions in home industries in Czechoslovakia, provides for the protection of the workmen's health and the regulation of working hours. It also provides for a minimum wage.

By the terms of the Act, the Minister of Social Welfare appoints a Central Commission for each branch of manufacture in which home work is carried on. It is the duty of these Central Commissions to fix minimum rates of wages for home workers and workshop assistants, and minimum prices for goods delivered by middlemen and home workers to contractors and intermediaries. It is also their duty to decide complaints against the decisions issued by the district commissions in their respective branches of manufacturing. They may also regulate in other respects conditions regarding work and the delivery of goods.

Contractors for whom goods are manufactured, intermediaries, and middlemen who employ home workers or workshop assistants must notify the competent industrial authority of the type of manufacture they are engaged in and must keep a list of the workers employed by them. This list is submitted to the industrial authority, the industrial and public health inspectors, and the sickness insurance funds concerned, on request. A list of minimum wage rates countersigned by the authorities must be permanently and visibly posted at every place where work is given out or handed in, or where wages are paid. Any person who gives out work directly to home workers must prepare for such workers a book containing the agreement concerning the calculation and the amount of wages, and also the wages actually paid.

6. COMPARISON WITH I.L.O. STANDARDS

Without the necessity of any changes in this legislation, Czechoslovakia on August 24, 1921, ratified the Convention limiting the hours of work in industrial undertakings to eight in the day and forty-eight in the week, adopted by the first session of the International Labor Conference in Washington in 1919, and on August 31, 1923, ratified the Convention concerning the application of the weekly rest in industrial undertakings adopted at the third session of the International Labor Conference at Geneva in 1921.[13]

The Hours Convention applies to " Industrial Undertakings ", which, according to Article 1, includes mines, manufacturing industries, construction works, and transportation. The Eight Hour Law as supplemented by the Circular of March 21, 1919, is of wider scope than the Convention, as it regulates the hours of work of all workers, manual and professional, regardless of status. It applies to all types of wage-earners, to agricultural workers, and to persons employed in domestic service. The two last named groups of workers are not covered by the Hours Convention.

Article 2 of the Convention states that when the hours of work on one or more days of the week are less than eight, the limit of eight hours may be exceeded on the remaining days of the week, provided that in no case " shall the daily limit of eight hours be exceeded by more than one hour." In the Eight Hour Law there is no such provision.

In Article 2 (c) of the Hours Convention, it states that " where persons are employed in shifts, it shall be permissible to employ persons in excess of eight hours in any one day and forty-eight hours in any one week, if the average number of hours over a period of three weeks or less does not exceed eight per day and forty-eight per week." The provisions of the Eight Hour Law are somewhat different in this respect, but the idea is the same. Under Hours of Work, Section 1, Sub-Section 5, the law provides that the Minister of Social Welfare in agreement with the Ministers concerned " may allow for particular groups of undertakings, especially transport and agricultural undertakings, an arrangement of hours of work differing from that prescribed in Sub-Section 1, provided that they shall not exceed 192 hours altogether within a period of four weeks." [14]

In regard to weekly rest in industrial undertakings, Article 2 of the Convention concerning weekly rest provides that " the whole of the staff employed in any industrial undertaking, public or private, or in any branch thereof, shall, except as otherwise provided for, enjoy in every period of seven days a period of rest comprising at least twenty-four consecutive hours." [15] The Eight Hour Law, under Breaks in Work, Section 4, Sub-Section 1, states that the worker must be allowed in every week an uninterrupted period of rest of at least thirty-two hours. The labor legislation of Czechoslovakia regarding hours of work and the weekly rest in industrial undertakings is therefore in harmony with the Hours Convention and, in the instances specified, the legislation of Czechoslovakia sets up higher standards than those of the Convention.

The Czechoslovak Government declared (1938) that it has under preparation an amendment of the legislation at present in force, with a view to bringing it into harmony with the provisions of the Hours of Work (Commerce and Offices) Convention, 1930.[16] Further, on February 25, 1938, the Council of Ministers approved bills for the ratification of the Sheet-Glass Workers Convention, 1935, as well as a bill for the enforcement of the provisions of these Conventions.[17] It is understood that legislation introducing the forty-two hour week in glass works is on the point of being adopted.

---

1 C. W. A. Veditz, *Child Labor Legislation in Europe* (Bulletin of Bureau of Labor, Dept. of Commerce and Labor, No. 89 [1910] Washington: Government Printing Office), pp. 3-92.

2 Percy Alden, Editor, *Hungary of Today* (London: E. Nash, 1909), p. 251.

3 *Legislative Series* (International Labor Office, Geneva, Switzerland, 1919), Cz. 1, p. 1.

4 *Ibid.*, p. 9.

5 *Legislative Series*, 1919, Cz. 1, p. 6.

6 *Industrial and Labor Information* (International Labor Office, Geneva, Switzerland, XLVII, 338; XLIX, 159.

7 *Ibid.*, XLVI, 148; LI, 200; LII, 302; LIV, 183, 257; LVI, 427.

8 See *supra*, p. 34.

9 *Industrial and Labor Information*, LI, 141.

10 *Ibid.*, LIV, 358.

11 *Ibid.*, LXIII, 279.

12 *Legislative Series*, 1920, Cz. 1.

13 See *infra*, pp. 147, 154.

14 For the text of the Hours Convention, see *Official Bulletin* (International Labor Office, Geneva, Switzerland, I, 409.

15 For the text of Convention concerning the application of the weekly rest, see *Official Bulletin*, IV, 503.

16 *Report of the Director*, Twenty-fourth Session, Geneva, 1938, p. 17.

17 *Ibid.*, p. 24, 27.

CHAPTER II

SPECIAL PROVISIONS FOR THE PROTECTION OF CHILDREN

A. In Austria Prior to 1918

During the eighteenth century the Austrian Government encouraged the employment of children as one of the means of developing the industries of the Empire. Even during this period, however, it was recognized that their employment involved certain dangers and evils. Hence the enactment during the eighteenth century of apprenticeship laws which provided that masters must not maltreat their young charges nor require them to perform work not connected with the trade they were learning.

In 1786 the impaired health and the wretched physical condition of children living in the apprentice homes connected with many factories led to an ordinance which declared that the dormitories for boys and girls must be separated; that every child should have a separate bed; and that clean bed linen must be provided every week. In 1816 the terms of this ordinance were reenacted and the municipal and circuit physicians were instructed to supervise the physical condition of factory children.

The detrimental effects of excessively long periods of work led to the Decree of 1787 which provided that factory children should receive instruction. This decree provided that children must not be employed in factories before their ninth year except in cases of necessity.

The first real child labor law in Austria was the Decree of June 11, 1842. According to this decree, no child under twelve years of age could be employed in a factory, but the local authorities were empowered to permit the employment of children nine years of age if they had completed three years of school attendance. Children nine to twelve years of age were not allowed to work more than ten hours a day. Those from twelve to sixteen years of age might work twelve hours a day. There must be at least one hour's rest during the workday. Night work, that is, work between 9 P.M. and 5 A.M., was forbidden to all persons under sixteen years of age. Employers were required to keep a list of their child laborers. Violations of the law were punishable by a fine of 2 to 100 gulden (.96 to $48.20). For repeated offenses, the right to employ children under twelve might be withdrawn. The enforcement of the law was intrusted to the local administrative authorities, to the district school superintendents, and to the local clergy.

The division of responsibility for enforcement of the law was unsatisfactory. Violations were frequent. Cotton mills were reported as employing children under eight years of age. The paper mills and cotton mills in 1845 contained 38,124 workers, of which 5,590 or 14.7 per cent were children of twelve years of age or less. In Vorarlberg, children seven and eight years old worked thirteen hours a day and three or four hours longer in times of exceptional industrial activity.

After an official investigation of the conditions in the factories engaged in the manufacture of matches, the Decree of September 3, 1846, was issued, prohibiting the employment of children in making phosphorus paste and in rooms in which the drying process was carried on. A further step was taken by the enactment of an Industrial Ordinance on December 20, 1859, which forbade the employment of children under ten years of age in larger industrial enterprises, namely, in those employing more than twenty workers. Children between ten and twelve years of age were allowed to work therein only when provided with a permit granted at the request of the child's parents or guardian by the local authorities. They could not be employed at work injurious to their health or apt to hinder their physical development. For persons under fourteen years of age the maximum workday was fixed at ten hours; for those between fourteen and sixteen, it was twelve hours. In both cases the workday should be interrupted by sufficient pauses for rest. Night work was forbidden persons under sixteen years of age, but in establishments operated both day and night and in which production would otherwise be seriously interfered with, the local authorities could permit night work for persons under sixteen, but not for those under fourteen years of age, on condition that the workers alternated between night work and day work. In times of great demand, the authorities might permit children under sixteen years of age to work two hours longer than the usual maximum for a period not exceeding four weeks.

The Imperial School Law of May 14, 1869, provided that when children employed in factories were unable to attend the commercial schools, employers must provide for their education in accordance with the standards established for public schools. In these factory schools, the hours of instruction must not fall below twelve hours per week and must be divided among the days of the week as equally as possible.

The Ordinance of 1859, combined with the School Law of 1869, constituted a step beyond previous legislation. But in the absence of any satisfactory provision for enforcement, the law remained practically a dead letter. The public officials intrusted with the execution of the school law and the industrial ordinance were already too heavily burdened with other tasks to give any attention to what took place in factories and workshops. It was not until the Law of June 17, 1883, providing for the appointment of special factory inspectors, was passed that any real effort was made to enforce the labor laws.

The Industrial Code of 1885, which was the law in force in Austria in 1914, provided that children under twelve years of age might not be employed regularly in industrial establishments. Those between twelve and fourteen years of age might be employed only to the extent that the labor in which they engaged was not detrimental to their health or to their physical development and did not interfere with their attendance at school during the period fixed by law. Furthermore, they could not work more than eight hours per day. The Minister of Commerce, in conjunction with the Minister of the Interior and with the advice of the chambers of commerce and industry, was empowered to issue ordinances designating the industrial occupations that involved danger to the life, limb, or health of those employed therein and in which women and children might therefore either not engage at all or only under certain specified conditions.

There was no general ordinance giving a list of these occupations. There were, however, several ordinances that were issued in conformity with Paragraph 74 of the Industrial Code, which concerned measures that must be taken to safeguard workers from industrial diseases and accidents. One of these ordinances, that of April 15, 1908, applied to persons engaged in painting and lacquering, and forbade the employment of children in the industrial use of white lead and lead compounds.

A law of July 28, 1902, forbade the employment of girls under sixteen at all, and of boys after 8 P.M. or before 6 A.M. in certain branches of railway service. It also forbade overtime work for boys under sixteen in the same occupations. Children under fourteen years of age might not peddle goods, and the employment of girls under eighteen at this occupation might be restricted or forbidden by the industrial authorities.

Children under sixteen years of age must not be employed at night, that is, between 8 P.M. and 5 A.M., in establishments subject to the law. But the Minister of Commerce, in consultation with the Minister of the Interior, was empowered to issue ordinances modifying this provision concerning night work or to exempt certain categories of occupations from compliance with it because of climatic circumstances or for other important reasons. He might permit the employment of children between fourteen and sixteen years of age at night in factories in which continuous operation was imperative or in which the temporary requirements of the industry made it necessary to employ alternating relays of workers. In conformity with the powers thus conferred upon the Minister of Commerce, the prohibition of night work for children was suspended in all industrial establishments engaged in certain specified industries.

By the Ordinance of June 8, 1907, children under fourteen years of age might not be employed as laborers in mines. But upon the petition of parents or guardians, the authorities might grant permission to employ children between twelve and fourteen years of age at light work above ground provided it did not interfere with the performance of their school duties. Laborers between fourteen and sixteen years of age might be employed only at work that was not beyond their strength and not injurious to their physical development. Girls under eighteen years of age might not be employed underground at all. Certain kinds of work, such as pushing wagons up slanting galleries and moving heavily loaded wagons, were specifically enumerated as forbidden for boys under sixteen and girls under eighteen years of age. Boys under sixteen years of age and girls under eighteen might not as a rule work between 8 P.M. and 5 A.M. But in mines employing two shifts per day, boys under sixteen might be employed until 11 P.M.

In cases of imminent danger to life, health, or property, children might be employed overtime or at night when adult laborers were not available for extra work under such circumstances. Boys under sixteen and girls under eighteen years of age must have regular pauses for rest amounting to at least one hour more than those allowed adult laborers. The pauses must be so arranged that no actual working period exceeded four hours. Any other arrangement was permissible only when made necessary by the operation of the mine or in the interest of the laborers themselves. Whenever young persons were employed on Sundays by way of exceptions provided by law, they must be given a compensatory day of rest during the week following. Exceptions to the legal provisions regarding night work, pauses, and length of the working period might be granted with regard to young persons of the male sex only when a physician acceptable to the authorities furnished a certificate indicating the kind of work in which it was proposed to employ the child and stating that such employment was neither detrimental to his physical development nor involved danger to his health.[1]

B. In Hungary Prior to 1918

In Hungary the Industrial Law of 1884 contained provisions for the protection of children in industry. According to this law, apprentices under fourteen years of age were restricted to a maximum workday of ten hours. For apprentices of fourteen years and over, the maximum number of hours was twelve daily, including hours of school attendance. Generally, they were to be employed only upon such work as would not interfere with their physical development. Intervals of half an hour at times before and after noon, and of a full hour at noon were provided for. Apprentices under sixteen were not as a rule to be employed upon night work, that is, between 9 P.M. and 5 A.M. In such industrial concerns as would suffer if night work were restricted, it might be allowed by the Industrial Authority for children between the ages of fourteen and sixteen.

The employment of children under ten was forbidden. Children between the ages of ten and twelve might be employed only by permission of the Industrial Authority. Such permission might be given only if regular school attendance was possible along with the employment. Between the ages of fourteen and sixteen, the maximum number of working hours was ten. In works reported as dangerous or unhealthy, workmen under sixteen years of age were either absolutely prohibited from working, or were allowed to do so only under certain conditions; and in any case, they might be employed only in such work as would not injure their health.[2]

C. In Czechoslovakia

The Act Respecting the Eight Hour Working Day contains a section on Young Persons in which it is stated that children shall not be employed in establishments in which the Industrial

Code applies, before the conclusion of their compulsory school attendance or before they are fourteen years of age. Male workers up to sixteen years of age and female workers up to eighteen years of age may be employed only on light work which is not injurious to their health and does not check their physical development. Only male workers may be employed in mines.

The child labor provisions of the Eight Hour Day Act were supplemented by the Act of July 17, 1919,[3] respecting child labor. In this Act, child labor is defined to mean the employment of children in any work whatever for which remuneration is paid or which is carried on regularly even if it is not specially remunerated. The scope of the Act of July 17, 1919 is therefore wider than that of the Act of December 19, 1918 which applied to the work of children only in undertakings subject to the Industrial Code or carried on as factories, in undertakings, works, and institutions carried on by the State, by public or private associations, funds, societies, or companies, to mining undertakings, and to the work of children regularly employed in agriculture and forestry who live outside the household of the employer and receive daily, weekly, or monthly wages. Employment of children exclusively for purposes of instruction or education is not held to be child labor; nor is the employment of children in isolated services or the employment of a person's own children in light work in the household held to be child labor.

By the terms of this Act, children may be employed only in work which does not injure their health or morals and which does not interfere with their compulsory school attendance. On school days, children may not be employed for more than two hours. Employment before morning school and during the two hours immediately preceding afternoon school is prohibited. In agriculture and domestic service, this prohibition is limited in general to the two hours immediately preceding afternoon school. After school, one hour's leisure must be allowed. On holidays, children are not to be employed for more than four hours or in agriculture and domestic work for more than six hours.

In agriculture and domestic service, children are to be allowed an uninterrupted night's rest of ten hours. The hours of the night's rest must be the hours between 8 P. M. and 6 A. M. The provincial governments may fix other limits as an exception to this rule, provided that the legally prescribed length of the night's rest is not reduced. In all other branches of child labor besides agriculture and domestic service, the employment of children between 8 P. M. and 7 A. M. is prohibited. Only male workers over sixteen years of age may be employed on night work.

A child may not be employed on Sundays nor on the church festivals celebrated by the denomination to which he belongs. Deviations from this provision are permitted in the case of work of a temporary nature which cannot be postponed and which must be undertaken in the public interest or on account of urgent necessity.

Children may not be employed in the following workplaces:

Places where distilled alcoholic drinks are served and sold retail; distilleries; beer, wine and other cellars; and breweries.

Workplaces for the preparation of slate goods, slates, and slate pencils, except workplaces where no processes are carried on other than coloring, painting and sticking, or the packing of slate pencils, and the coloring, ruling, and framing of school slates.

Stone quarries and pits.

Stone-masons', stone-cutters', stone-borers', stone-polishers' workshops.

Brick works, plaster works, timber yards.

Lime burning, plaster burning.

Workplaces for the manufacture and decoration of earthenware pots, vessels, and tiles.

Glass-blowers', glass-etchers', glass-polishers', glass-annealers' workshops, with the exception of glass-blowing workplaces in which glass-blowing at the lamp alone is carried on.

Works for the silvering of mirrors.

Workplaces where articles are glazed, given a metal coating by galvanic means through gilding, plating, nickeling, etc., or in which articles are prepared by the galvanaplastic method.

Workplaces where lead and tin toys are painted; lead, zinc, tin, copper, and brass casting shops and other metal-casting shops.

Hook makers' and bronzers' workshops.

Workplaces in which lead, copper, zinc, or alloys of these metals are prepared or used.

Metal-polishing, file-cutting, harness-making, lead-soldering works.

Fringe-knotting works.

Workplaces in which mercury is used.

Workplaces in which lead or lead compounds are made, prepared, or used.

Workplaces for the preparation of explosives, fireworks, matches, and other inflammable substances.

Workplaces where celluloid goods are made.

Chemical works.

Flaying houses.

Workplaces in which spun or woven materials are bleached by means of chemicals, and dye works.

Rag sorting workshops.

Leather curing and leather dressing works, tanneries.

Workplaces for the preparation of india-rubber and gutta-percha goods.

Horsehair spinning works, fur-cutting works, and other workplaces in which animal hair is prepared.

Hair and bristle-dressing works, brush, and paint-brush works.

Workplaces for the preparation of mother-of-pearl.

Bakeries.

Slaughter-houses.

Works for cleaning bed feathers.

Chemical cleaning works.

Painters', house-painters', decorators and lacquerers' work-places.

Livery stables.

Turners' shops.

Mills.

Chimney-sweeping businesses.

Child labor is also prohibited in the following kinds of work:

Tending power machines and all machines, shafting, and lifts driven by motor-power.

Working machines driven by hand, except winding with common hand-winders, or spooling-wheels, and tending so-called spinning machines for the making of artificial flowers and cotton-wool fruit.

Employment in connection with winches and other similar dangerous machines and appliances.

Employment in connection with straw and fodder cutting machines.

Employment in building and earth works.

Tending apparatus in which there are liquids, steam, or gases under pressure.

Oven and furnace work.

Processes in which dust or gas is generated.

Collecting or sorting of rags.

Mixing or grinding of colors.

Work in beer, wine, and other cellars.

Stone-breaking.

Lifting, carrying, and moving heavy weights.

Woodfelling and chopping.

Threshing.

Reaping.

Helping in hunting.

Drawing nets in fishing.

Industrial employers who employ young persons as wage earners must keep registers showing the name, age, and address of these workers, their parents' or guardians' address, and the date of their entering or leaving employment. Employers must show these registers on request to the administrative authorities of first instance. In undertakings employing more than thirty wage earners, the works council may ask once a year for a list of all the persons employed in the undertaking, together with their dates of birth.

By virtue of this legislation, Czechoslovakia, on August 24, 1921, ratified the Convention fixing the minimum age for admission of children to industrial employment, adopted by the International Labor Conference at its first session in Washington, in 1919, and on May 14, 1924, ratified the Convention concerning the age for admission of children to employment in agriculture, adopted at the third session of the International Labor Conference at Geneva in 1921. Article 2 of the former states that "children under the age of fourteen years shall not be employed or work in any public or private industrial undertaking, or in any branch thereof, other than an undertaking in which only members of the same family are employed."[4] This coincides exactly with the provision in Section 10 of the Eight Hour Day Law which states that in the undertakings named in Section 1 (which includes all public and private industrial undertakings, mining, and regular employment in agriculture, and forestry where the worker lives outside the household of the employer and receives daily, weekly, or monthly wages), children shall not be employed before the conclusion of their compulsory school attendance, and before they are fourteen years of age.

Article 1 of the latter states that children under the age of fourteen years may not be employed or work in any public or private agricultural undertaking or in any branch thereof, save outside the hours fixed for school attendance. If they are employed outside the hours of school attendance, the employment shall not be such as to prejudice their attendance at school.

Article 2 provides that, for purposes of practical vocational instruction, the periods and the hours of school attendance may be so arranged as to permit the employment of children on light agricultural work, and in particular on light work connected with the harvest, provided that such employment shall not reduce the total annual period of school attendance to less than eight months. Article 3 states that the provisions of Article 1 shall not apply to work done by children in technical schools, provided that such work is approved and supervised by public authority.[5]

Section 1 of the Act respecting child labor of July 17, 1919, states that children under fourteen years of age shall be employed or otherwise occupied only in pursuance of this act. Section 4 states that children shall be employed or otherwise occupied only in so far as their health is not injured thereby, or their physical or mental development, or their morals endangered, and provided that they are not thereby prevented from carrying out their compulsory school attendance. No child shall be employed under the age of twelve years. Notwithstanding, children may be employed on light work in agriculture and domestic work as soon as they attain the age of ten years. Section 5 states that on school days, children may not be employed for more than two hours; employment before morning school and during the two hours immediately preceding afternoon school is prohibited. The provision in respect of employment before morning school does not apply to agriculture and domestic work. After school, one hour's leisure shall be allowed.

Czechoslovakia has not ratified the Convention concerning the night work of young persons employed in industry adopted by the International Labor Conference at its first session in Washington in 1919. Article 2 of this Convention prohibits the employment of children under eighteen years of age in industrial enterprises during the night.[6] Section 9 of the Czechoslovak Eight Hour Day Law forbids the employment at night of women under eighteen years of age, but it admits night work in the case of males over sixteen years of age. It would be necessary to change this age limit to eighteen years to bring the law of Czechoslovakia into conformity with the standards of the Convention. Although attempts have been made to bring about this change, the records up to January 1938 do not show that it has been accomplished.[7] This illustrates the policy of Czechoslovakia not to ratify Conventions until her laws are in conformity with the standards set up by them.

---

1 C. W. A. Veditz, *Child-Labor Legislation in Europe*, pp. 3-19.

2 Percy Alden, Editor, *Hungary of Today*, p. 248.

3 *Legislative Series*, 1920, Cz. 2.

4 For the text of the Convention fixing the minimum age for admission of children to industrial employment, see *Official Bulletin*, I, 430.

5 For the text of the Convention concerning the age for admission of children to employment in agriculture, see *Official Bulletin*, IV, 490.

6 For the text of the Convention concerning the night work of young persons employed in industry, see *Official Bulletin*, I, 433.

7 See *infra*, p. 151.

CHAPTER III

SPECIAL PROVISIONS FOR THE PROTECTION OF WOMEN

A. In Austria Prior to 1918

Austria ratified the International Agreement of September 26, 1906, respecting the prohibition of night work of women in industrial occupations on February 1, 1911, and on February 21, 1911, passed the Act relating to the prohibition of the night work of women in industrial undertakings.[1] This act provided that in the case of industrial undertakings where more than ten workers were employed, no women or girls might be employed at night, that is, during the hours between 8 P.M. and 5 A.M. The time set apart for night rest should amount to at least eleven consecutive hours. All industrial undertakings and building operations were included in the act, but agriculture and forestry were excluded. In unforeseen cases of interruption of work, which did not occur periodically, the prohibition of the night work of those female workers who had completed their eighteenth year might be dispensed with. Should this unexpected work exceed eight days in duration, the consent of the political authority of first instance was necessary, which consent, however, could not be accorded for more than four weeks.

This act also allowed the Minister of Commerce to indicate by order those industrial undertakings in which, during the working-up of raw material or the treatment of substances which were subject to rapid deterioration, the prohibition of night work did not apply to female workers over eighteen years of age. The duration of the uninterrupted night's rest in the case of those branches of industry which were affected by the seasons might be reduced to ten hours for a maximum of forty days in the year. Also, this night rest might be made to commence at ten o'clock for female workers over eighteen.

An Ordinance of April 15, 1908, forbade the employment of women in painting and lacquering establishments where white lead and lead compounds were used. Several other ordinances adopted in the Austrian provinces before 1914 and several ordinances adopted for those provinces called "historical territories," or for Slovakia and sub-Carpathian Russia, protect women against employment in unhealthy and exhausting work—printing and building trades, quarries, etc.

The Act of December 26, 1911, modified and supplemented the provisions of the Act of June 21, 1884, regarding the employment of women in mines.[2] It provided that women and girls of whatever age might not be employed underground in the mining industry, and that mothers should not be employed until six weeks after their confinement. Women and girls might not be employed during the night, that is, between the hours of 8 P. M. and 5 A. M. Permission for exemptions might be given only to women and girls who had passed their eighteenth year, and on the condition that the night rest was of at least eleven hours' duration. Overtime work might be undertaken only by women who had passed their eighteenth year, and only on forty days during the year, on the condition that the night rest was of at least ten hours' duration.[3]

By the Act of May 13, 1912, it was decreed that "quarries should be reckoned under all circumstances amongst those industrial undertakings to which the Act of Feb. 21, 1911 applied."[4]

B. In Hungary Prior to 1918

According to the Hungarian law of August 14, 1911,[5] women employed in industrial undertakings employing more than ten workers, should, with certain exceptions, be granted an uninterrupted night's rest of at least eleven hours. Women might not be employed between the hours of 10 P. M. and 5 A. M. These regulations regarding the night rest of women did not apply to agriculture, to undertakings where only members of the family were employed, to restaurants and coffee-houses, to the administration and working of railways and navigation undertakings, postal telegraph, and telephone service of the state, nor to undertakings which were carried on during certain seasons only.

By the Order of January 5, 1912,[6] the employment of women in mining and smelting works was prohibited between the hours of 10 P.M. and 5 A.M. An uninterrupted interval of night rest of at least eleven hours should be granted to the women employed. This night rest should comprise the time from 10 P.M. to 5 A.M.

C. In Czechoslovakia

The Act Respecting the Eight Hour Day, in Section 9, provides that women shall not be employed on night work. However, the Minister of Social Welfare may designate those groups of undertakings and industries in which the night work of women over eighteen may be allowed as an exception and for a short period, in the preparation of raw materials and substances liable to rapid deterioration. In addition, the Minister of Social Welfare may allow specified groups of undertakings to employ women over eighteen at night between the hours of 10 P.M. and 5 A.M. if this is necessary for the uninterrupted progress of the undertaking or out of special consideration for public interests, and if the work of the women consists of operations demanding comparatively little exertion.

The Act also provides that women may not be employed in mines, including surface works. Furthermore, it provides that the uninterrupted period of rest of at least thirty-two hours per week may not begin later than 2 o'clock on Saturday afternoon in the case of women employed in factories. However, the Minister of Social Welfare was empowered to grant exceptions to this rule within the limits of the prescribed weekly hours of work for any undertaking in which the employment of women is essential to the progress of the undertaking.

By the Order of January 11, 1919, the Minister of Social Welfare granted permission for the night work of women over eighteen years of age during the season in the manufacture of jam and fruit pulp and in the drying of vegetables and fruit. In addition, permission was granted for women over eighteen years of age to be employed at night, that is, between 10 P.M. and 5 A.M., in agricultural undertakings, dairies, hotels, booking offices of transport undertakings, telephone and telegraph service, the delivery of newspapers, theatres, places of amusement, and hospitals.

On August 24, 1921, Czechoslovakia ratified the Convention concerning the employment of women during the night, adopted by the International Labor Conference at its first session in Washington in 1919. Article 3 of this Convention provides that women, without distinction of age, shall not be employed during the night in any public or private industrial undertaking, or in any branch thereof, other than an undertaking in which only members of the same family are employed. Article 4 states that this restriction shall not apply in cases of " force majeure ", when in any undertaking there occurs an interruption of work which it was impossible to foresee and which is not of a recurring character. Neither shall it apply in cases where the work has to do with raw materials or materials in course of treatment which are subject to rapid deterioration when such night work is necessary to preserve the said materials from certain loss.[7]

It is obvious that Czechoslovak legislation is in harmony with the terms of the Convention, as it prohibits night work of women in general but makes exceptions for a short period in the preparation of raw materials and in undertakings vested with a public interest.

Czechoslovakia did not ratify the Convention concerning the employment of women before and after childbirth, which was also adopted at the first session of the International Labor Conference in Washington in 1919. Article 3 of this Convention states that in any public or private industrial or commercial undertaking, or in any branch thereof, other than an undertaking in which only members of the same family are employed, a woman—

(a) Shall not be permitted to work during the six weeks following her confinement.

(b) Shall have the right to leave her work if she produces a medical certificate stating that her confinement will probably take place within six weeks.

(c) Shall, while she is absent from her work, be paid benefits sufficient for the full and healthy maintenance of herself and her child, provided either out of public funds or by means of a system of insurance, the exact amount of which shall be determined by the competent authority in each country and as an additional benefit, shall be entitled to free attendance by a doctor or certified midwife.[8]

The Czechoslovak Act respecting the Eight Hour Day says nothing about the employment of women before and after childbirth. In the several Sickness Insurance Acts of 1924-36, the employment of women was prohibited only for the six weeks after childbirth. It was left to the discretion of the Sickness Benefit Institutions to make special provision for women before confinement. However, it was provided that a woman should receive assistance equivalent to the ordinary rates of sick benefit for six weeks before and for six weeks after childbirth if the insured woman abstained from paid work.[9] Also, insured women who nurse their children have a further claim for a nursing allowance which is half the sick benefit and is payable for twelve weeks following childbirth. The sickness funds set up by the Sickness Insurance Act offer not only to all female employees (including agricultural employees), but also to her family dependents for the whole length of the confinement period, and in case of a protracted invalidity even for a longer term, medical and obstetrical assistance with the necessary medicines, besides the subsidies to which the insured workers is entitled during her illness. Article 4 of the Convention states that if a woman is absent from her work in accordance with Paragraphs (a) and (b) of Article 3, or remains absent from her work for a longer period as a result of illness medically certified to arise out of pregnancy or confinement and rendering her unfit for work, it is not lawful, until her absence exceeds a maximum period fixed by the competent authority, for her employer to give her notice of dismissal during such absence, nor to give her notice of dismissal at such a time that the notice would expire during such absence. Czechoslovak legislation does not provide for leave of absence with maintenance of the right or re-employment during the whole period of absence.

In 1920, a bill providing for the changes necessary to bring Czechoslovak legislation into conformity with the childbirth Convention was drafted by the Minister of Social Welfare and placed before the National Assembly for consideration. To date, June 1938, the records do not show that any action has been taken on this bill.[10] This is another illustration of the policy of Czechoslovakia not to ratify Conventions until her laws are in accord with the standards set up by them.

---

1 *Bulletin of the International Labor Office*, Basle, Switzerland, (London: Labor Representation Printing and Publishing Co., Ltd., 1911), VI [1911], 118.

2 *Op. cit.*, VII [1912], 12.

3 According to information from unofficial sources, several other Ordinances were adopted in the Austrian provinces before 1914 to protect women against employment in unhealthy and exhausting work.

4 *Op. cit.*, VIII [1913], 251.

5 *Op. cit.*, VII [1912], p. 211.

6 *Ibid.*, VIII [1913], p. 23.

7 For the text of the Convention concerning employment of women during the night, see *Official Bulletin*, I, 424.

8 For the text of the Convention concerning the employment of women before and after childbirth, see *Official Bulletin*, I, 421.

9 See *infra*, pp. 66-71. The Sickness Insurance Acts do not prohibit employment. Employment is, however, prohibited for the six weeks succeeding confinement by the Industrial Code [former Austrian Code, Par. 94] which applies in Bohemia, Moravia, and Silesia, and by Par. 131 of a similar act adopted Oct. 10, 1934 for the provinces of Slovakia and sub-Carpathian Russia.

10 See *infra*, pp. 149-151.

PART II

SOCIAL INSURANCE

CHAPTER IV

SICKNESS INSURANCE

A. In Austria Prior to 1918

Sickness insurance in Austria was based on the law of March 30, 1888 [1] as amended by the Acts of Apr. 4, 1899, Feb. 8, 1909, Feb. 11, 1913, and Jan. 4, 1917. Sickness and accident insurance were closely united by the provisions of the Sickness Insurance law as amended, so that the persons subject to the compulsory accident insurance are also subject to the compulsory sickness insurance.

1. SCOPE

The industries included in the insurance were:

a. The factory and smelting industries, mining, shipyards, quarries, establishments using or manufacturing explosives, and all classes of establishments in which power was used.

b. Building trades and operations connected therewith.

c. Establishments subject to the provisions of the Industrial Code, as well as other business undertakings.

d. Railway and other transportation and inland navigation.

Sickness insurance did not cover home industries, agriculture, or forestry. However, any establishment in these industries might be included in the insurance, if the employer and his employees so desired. The group of industries which were subject to the compulsory sickness insurance because they were included under the provisions of the Industrial Code comprised a great variety of establishments. In general, the Industrial Code regulated all enterprises carried on as a business which were engaged in the production, working up, or transforming of articles of commerce, enterprises engaged in commerce, or enterprises for the rendering of services (messenger service, etc.). Under the term "other business undertakings", were included such establishments as pharmacies, pawnshops, notaries' offices, private educational and training institutions, private post-offices, tobacco shops, stores of cooperative societies even if not conducted for profit, savings and credit banks, insurance companies, theatres, etc.

The classes of persons subject to the compulsory sickness insurance were workmen and administrative officials. These included apprentices, voluntary workers, and other persons who received either no wage or only partial wages because of their unfinished period of training. All workmen were subject to the compulsory insurance, regardless of the amount of their earnings. Administrative officials of an establishment, however, were included in the compulsory insurance if their annual earnings were less than 2,400 crowns ($487.20). In case their earnings exceeded this amount, they might insure themselves voluntarily, and, like other persons so insured, must pay the entire amount of the dues themselves.

2. ADMINISTRATION

The administration of the compulsory sickness insurance law was in the hands of sickness insurance associations or funds, based on geographical lines, one compulsory insurance fund being created for each geographical subdivision of the country. These organizations were not state institutions, but independent associations, managed by their own members though subject to the supervision of state officials. The membership in each district sickness fund consisted of all insured persons employed in the territory of the district who were not members of other funds. The board of directors of the district sickness fund was elected by the general meeting of the members from their own number. This board conducted the business of the fund and exercised all of the powers of the fund. In particular, the board exercised an effective control over the claims of members for sickness benefits.

3. FINANCIAL RESOURCES

The means for the support of the various sickness funds were procured by assessments levied in the form of a percentage of the wages of the insured person. The latter paid two-thirds and the employers paid one-third of the rate fixed by the fund to which the workman belonged. The workman's share was deducted from his wages by the employer who transmitted it to the fund together with his own dues. The employer was not allowed to deduct any part of his share of the dues from the wages of the workman.

4. BENEFITS

Insurance covered the risks of sickness, maternity, and death.

a. *Sickness*

Insured persons were entitled to the following benefits:

1. From the beginning of the sickness, free medical treatment, as well as free medicines, and therapeutical appliances (eyeglasses, crutches, etc.).

2. In case the sickness lasted more than three days and the sick person was unable to work, he was paid for each day from the date of the beginning of the sickness a sick benefit equal in amount to 60 per cent of the current rate of wages for ordinary day laborers in that district. The sick benefit was to be paid for a period of twenty weeks.

3. Instead of the free medical treatment, free medicines, and sick benefit, the sick person might receive free treatment and support in a hospital at the expense of the sick fund.

b. *Maternity*

Medical treatment included lying-in treatment. In cases of normal childbirth, the sick benefit was to be paid for at least four weeks after delivery.

c. *Death*

In case of death, the heirs should be paid a funeral benefit of not less than 20 times the rate of wages for ordinary day labor. The benefit was paid if the death occurred after the twenty weeks, provided that the sick person had retained his membership in the sick fund by continuing the payment of dues. If the disability was caused by an accident covered by the accident insurance laws, the funeral benefits might be claimed from both the sickness fund and from the accident insurance institution.

B. In Hungary Prior to 1918

Hungary, like Austria, took up the question of workmen's sickness insurance at an early date, treating it on the model of the German system of obligatory insurance. The Law of 1891 stated that the following employees must belong to some sick aid organization if their pay did not exceed four florins per day, or if they were not engaged for a shorter time than eight days: all those employees working at occupations coming within the Industrial Code, in mines, forges, or other concerns working up mine products; in quarries, and sand gravel beds; in the larger buildings, in railway works, and in post and telegraph offices; in navigation and shipbuilding; in carting and transport; and in warehouses and commercial establishments.

The wage was the standard upon which the contribution was based and the contribution amounted to not less than two and not more than four per cent of the wages paid. Two-thirds of this contribution must be paid by the employee and the remainder by the employer. The sick aid organizations had to provide the subscriber with medical help for a period not exceeding twenty weeks, and in case of confinement, with the necessary assistance and medical treatment, together with medicine and money for sustenance. In case of death, twenty times the amount of the subscription was to be given as burial aid. The sum for sustenance might not exceed seventy-five per cent of the wages calculated upon the basis of the amount of contribution. Sick aid could not be prolonged beyond one year. Only the insured members of a family could partake of free medical aid and medicine.

The law differentiated six kinds of sick aid organizations: district organizations upon which the most stress was laid; those of employees of businesses and factories; those of building employees; of industrial corporations; of mines, and finally, the sick aid organizations established by private bodies. The establishment of so many different kinds of such organizations was a disadvantage in so far as it led to the weakening of their financial position. The greater number of the organizations were constantly struggling with financial difficulties. Not only were they unable to meet payments above the minimum prescribed by law, but very often the minimum itself was paid with the greatest difficulty. Those district organizations which were spread over many parishes were unable to discharge their obligations over their whole area and very often limited their sphere of activity to the chief center and one or two of the larger towns. Therefore, sick aid hardly existed so far as most parishes were concerned.

The Law of 1907 was passed to reform sick aid procedure. The chief feature of this reform was the centralization and national organization of sick aid. The Workmen's National Sick Aid and Accident Insurance Society, created by this law, made for centralization in so far as it maintained the sole direction of sick aid matters throughout the whole country. The law also set up the State Workmen's Insurance Office, the duty of which was to superintend the sick aid organizations and their functions. The law recognized only the district and business sick aid organizations, ignoring the other classes enumerated in the previous law.

As regards compulsory insurance, the law widened its sphere. It not only extended over such occupations as came within the Industrial Code, but also to all employees in concerns carried on along industrial lines. The law also extended the obligation to insure to occupations not of an industrial nature, or to the employees thereof, who because of the temporary nature of their work or of the wage conditions could not, from the point of view of public health, be left out.

The law fixed the ratio of contributions for sick aid at half and half as between employer and employee. Sick aid lasted for ten weeks only, and during this time the worker received medical treatment, all medicines, and other medical appliances necessary for his treatment.[2]

C. In Czechoslovakia

In Czechoslovakia, the compulsory sickness insurance of workers and salaried employees is governed by the Act of October 9, 1924,[3] as amended by the Act of November 8, 1928 and by the Act of July 25, 1934[4] which codified and consolidated the entire system, while the special scheme for miners is governed by the Act of July 11, 1922 as amended by the Act of July 3, 1936,[5] and the sickness insurance of public employees is governed by the Act of October 15, 1925.[6] These acts are based to some extent on the old Austrian Act of March 30, 1888, and the old Hungarian Act No. XIX of 1907, but in letter and in spirit the Czechoslovak legislation is very different from that of the former Austro-Hungarian legislation.

1. Workers' and Salaried Employees' Insurance

a. *Scope.*

Workers' insurance is compulsory for every person who performs work or renders service under a contract of employment, service, or apprenticeship. It is also compulsory for home workers who, while not running a business, regularly exercise a trade at the order or on behalf of one or more employers. It does not apply to subsidiary or casual employment.

Salaried employees' insurance is compulsory for non-manual workers employed in private undertakings.

b. *Administration*

Compulsory sickness insurance is administered by institutions of various types. These include: district institutions, agricultural institutions, establishment institutions, association institutions, occupational guild institutions, and registered friendly society institutions.

Some salaried employees are insured with the workers' insurance institutions, the others belonging to institutions specially set up for the insurance of salaried employees. The sickness insurance institutions are managed by the general delegate meeting, the managing committee (three-fourths of which is made up of representatives of the insured persons and one-quarter of representatives of the employers), and a supervisory committee, of which three-fourths of the members are employers' representatives and one-fourth representatives of the insured persons. The supervision of the sickness insurance institutions is entrusted to the Central Social Insurance Institution.

c. *Financial Resources*

The money required to cover the cost of benefits, administrative expenses, and the accumulation of a reserve fund is derived from contributions, the rate of which is fixed for each sickness insurance institution by the Central Social Insurance Institution. As a rule, the contributions must not exceed 5.5 per cent of the average daily wage. The insured persons are classified in ten wage classes according to their wages (salaried employees in fifteen classes). The average wage of each class is fixed by law. Half the insurance contribution is borne by the employer and half by the insured person. The employer pays the whole of the insurance contribution for workers who receive no cash wages.

d. *Benefits*

Insurance covers the risks of sickness, maternity, and death.

1. Sickness

Insured persons are entitled to the following benefits:

(a) free medical treatment and drugs for themselves and the members of their family living in the same household, from the beginning of the sickness until it ends;

(b) daily sickness benefit as from the fourth day of working incapacity, for a period not exceeding one year. The rate of benefit varies with the wage class and is, as a rule, equivalent to about two-thirds of the average daily wage.

2. Maternity

Maternity benefits are as follows:

(a) obstetrical treatment (free service of a midwife and, if necessary, medical treatment) for insured women and wives of insured persons;

(b) daily benefit equal to the daily sickness benefit for insured women for six weeks before and six weeks after confinement;

(c) a nursing bonus, equal to half the daily sickness benefit, for mothers who nurse their children themselves, up to the end of the twelfth week after confinement.

3. Death

In case of the death of an insured person, funeral benefit is granted, equal to thirty times the daily wage of the insured person, with a minimum of 150 crowns. In case of the death of a member of the family, the insured person receives an allowance fixed at 60, 180, or 250 crowns, respectively, according to whether the deceased person was under two, under fourteen, or over fourteen years of age. Treatment in a hospital with full maintenance there may be substituted for sickness benefit and medical treatment. During this period the sick person is entitled to an allowance equal to half the sickness benefit which is paid to his family.

2. SPECIAL SCHEME FOR MINERS

a. *Scope*

Sickness insurance is compulsory for all persons employed in mining undertakings irrespective of age, sex, or nationality.

b. *Administratoin*

This insurance scheme is administered by eight benefit societies, one for the area of each district mining authority. The organs of the district societies consist of the general meeting, the managing committee, and the supervisory committee, all of which are composed of representatives elected by the insured persons and their employers.

c. *Financial Rcsources*

The money required to cover the cost of benefits, administrative expenses, and the accumulation of a reserve fund is derived from contributions payable in equal parts by the insured persons and their employers. The weekly contribution must not exceed four-tenths of the average daily wage of the wage class to which the miner belongs; but when necessary, it may be increased to a maximum of 8 per cent of the average daily wage. This increase must be authorized by the Minister of Public Works.

d. *Benefits*

Insurance covers the risks of sickness, maternity, and death.

1. Sickness

Insured persons are entitled to the following benefits:

(a) free medical treatment and drugs for themselves, and, when their income does not exceed 20,000 crowns a year, also for the members of their family living in the same household;

(b) daily sickness benefit, fixed in accordance with the wage class to which the insured person belongs, and generally equal to two-thirds of the average daily wage, for a maximum period of one year.

2. Maternity

Maternity benefits are as follows:

(a) obstetrical treatment (the free services of a midwife and, if necessary, of a doctor) for insured women and wives of insured persons;

(b) daily cash benefit equal to the sickness benefit for insured women for six weeks before and six weeks after confinement;

(c) a nursing bonus, equal to half the daily sickness benefit, for mothers who nurse their children themselves, up to the end of the twelfth week after confinement.

3. Death

In case of the death of an insured person, funeral benefit is granted equal to thirty times the average daily wage, with a minimum of 150 crowns. In case of the death of a member of the family, the insured person receives an allowance for funeral expenses, amounting to 60, 180, or 250 crowns, respectively, according to whether the deceased person was under two, under fourteen, or over fourteen years of age.

3. INSURANCE OF PUBLIC EMPLOYEES

a. *Scope*

Insurance is compulsory for the following persons:

1. civilian employees in the service of the State, State undertakings, or public funds administered by the State, and also members of the police forces;
2. teachers in elementary and secondary schools;
3. persons in the employment of a province, a union of counties, a county, a district, or a commune, or of the funds and institutions administered by them;
4. persons who are in receipt of ordinary pensions or superannuation allowances from the State, a province, a union of counties, a county, a district, or a commune, or from funds and institutions administered by them;

5. employees of the bodies corporate which are declared by the Ministry of Social Welfare to be in the same position as employees of the State and other compulsory territorial associations.

b. *Administration*

The insurance scheme is administered by the Medical Fund for Public Employees with headquarters in Prague. The administrative bodies of the Medical Fund are the Central Committee and its executive and the district committees. The Central Committee consists of twenty-four representatives of the insured persons, and four representatives of the Government. The executive consists of the chairman, two vice-chairmen, and two other members of the Central Committee. For the area of every district office, there is a district committee consisting of five members elected by the insured persons.

c. *Financial Resources*

The sums required for covering insurance benefits are raised by means of insurance contributions, which amount to 2 per cent of the regular salary, pension, or superannuation allowance. Half the insurance contribution is borne by the employer and half by the employee. The employer pays the whole of the insurance contribution for employees who receive no money wages (voluntary workers, candidates for employment, and persons undergoing training).

d. *Benefits*

Insurance covers medical treatment at home and institutional treatment. Every insured person is entitled to medical attendance, including attendance in confinement and the services of a midwife, medicines and other therapeutical requisites, and medical treatment for the members of his family. Treatment and maintenance in a hospital or other curative institution may be granted free of charge. In such case, the sick person is conveyed to the hospital and back to his home free of charge.

4. COMPARISON OF SICKNESS INSURANCE LEGISLATION IN CZECHOSLOVAKIA WITH I.L.O. STANDARDS

On January 17, 1929, Czechoslovakia ratified the Convention concerning sickness insurance for workers in industry and commerce and domestic servants, adopted by the International Labor Conference at its tenth session at Geneva in 1927. A survey of the main provisions of this Convention will show that the standards set up therein are similar to those set up by the sickness insurance legislation of Czechoslovakia.

Article 2 of this Convention states that the compulsory sickness insurance system shall apply to manual and non-manual workers, including apprentices, employed by industrial undertakings and commercial undertakings, out-workers, and domestic servants. Exceptions may be made for casual workers, workers whose wages exceed a certain amount, workers who are not paid a money wage, out-workers, workers below or above age-limits, and members of the employer's family. Article 3 provides for a cash benefit for at least the first twenty-six weeks of incapacity, with a waiting period of not more than three days. Article 4 provides for medical treatment and the supply of proper medicine and appliances, which according to Article 5 may also be granted to members of an insured person's family living in his household and dependent upon him. Article 6 states that sickness insurance shall be administered by self-governing institutions which shall be under the supervision of the competent public authority and shall not be carried on with a view of profit. The insured persons shall participate in the management of these insurance institutions. Article 7 states that the insured persons and their employers shall share in providing the financial resources of the sickness insurance system.[7]

On the same day, January 17, 1929, Czechoslovakia also ratified the Convention concerning sickness insurance for agricultural workers, which was also adopted by the International Labor Conference at its tenth session at Geneva in 1927. The provisions of this Convention are the same as those of the preceding Convention except that these apply to manual and non-manual workers, including apprentices, employed by agricultural undertakings.[8] The sickness insurance legislation of Czechoslovakia applies to agricultural as well as to industrial laborers.

---

1 *Bulletin of International Labor Office*, Basle, Switzerland, VIII [1913], 257; XII [1917], 51; Twenty-fourth Annual Report of Commissioner of Labor (Washington: Government Printing Office, 1911), I, 225.

2 Percy Alden, Editor, *Hungary of Today*, pp. 243-246.

3 *Legislative Series*, 1924, Cz. 4.

4 *Ibid.*, 1928, Cz. 2; 1934, Cz. 4.

5 *Ibid.*, 1922, Cz. 2; 1936, Cz. 5; I. L. O. Year-Book 1935-1936, p. 230; 1936-1937, p. 234.

6 *Ibid.*, 1925, Cz. 5.

7 For the text of the Convention concerning sickness insurance for workers in industry and commerce and domestic servants, see *Official Bulletin*, XII, 125.

8 For text of the Convention concerning sickness insurance for agricultural workers, see *Official Bulletin*, XII, 131.

CHAPTER V

OLD-AGE AND INVALIDITY, WIDOWS' AND ORPHANS' INSURANCE AND PENSIONS

A. In Austria Prior to 1918

An act was passed in Austria on December 16, 1906,[1] providing for the invalidity and old-age insurance of employees in private service and of certain employees in public service. Insured under the terms of this act were employees in private service who had completed their eighteenth year, who received a monthly or yearly salary, and whose earnings in the service of one employer amounted to at least 600 crowns per year. Also included under the terms of the act were those employees in the public service who had no established claim to disablement and old-age pensions. The act did not apply to employees in the service of the Court, of the State or of a State institution.

Within the meaning of this act, employees were all persons appointed to posts having an official character and, in general, all persons whose duties were of a more or less intellectual character. The following persons were not considered employees under the terms of the act: (1) persons directly employed in the manufacture of articles or in other labor mainly of a physical nature, that is, workmen, apprentices, or servants engaged in industry, mining, agriculture, and forestry; (2) persons who were engaged, wholly or mainly, in domestic service.

Persons covered by the insurance were arranged, according to the amounts of their annual earnings, in six classes ranging from Class 1, which included those receiving a yearly salary of from 600 to 900 crowns, to Class 6, which included those receiving over 3000 crowns per year.[2]

The following benefits were provided: (1) for the person insured, a disability or old-age annuity in case of incapacity for earning a living; (2) for dependents, an annuity for the widow, maintenance grants for the children, and final settlement of claim of dependents. Claims to benefits were not considered, unless payment of contributions had been made for a period of not less than one hundred and twenty months.

B. In Hungary Prior to 1918

There was no legislation in Hungary regarding old-age, invalidity, and widows' and orphans' insurance.

C. In Czechoslovakia

In Czechoslovakia, invalidity, old-age, and widows' and orphans' insurance is compulsory for three groups of persons. The insurance of workers is governed by the Act of October 9, 1924, as amended by the Act of November 8, 1928 and the Act of July 25, 1934.[3] The insurance of salaried employees is governed by the Act of February 21, 1929, amended by the Acts of July 14, 1931, and June 21, 1934.[4] The insurance of miners is governed by the Act of July 11, 1922 as amended by the Act of July 3, 1936.[5]

1. WORKERS' INSURANCE

a. *Scope*

Insurance is compulsory for all persons in the Czechoslovak Republic who perform work or render service under a contract of work, service, or apprenticeship which is not of a subsidiary or casual nature. Home workers are also liable to compulsory insurance.

b. *Administration*

The insurance scheme is administered by the Central Social Insurance Institution at Prague, which is alone competent to deal with workers' invalidity, old-age, and widows' and orphans' insurance. The chairman of the Institution is appointed by the Head of the State. The principal organ of the Institution is the committee, which is composed of forty members, including twelve representatives of the insured persons, twelve representatives of the employers, and sixteen social insurance experts appointed by the Government. The governing body of the Institution comprises ten members, including three elected by the insured persons' group of the committee, three elected by the employers' group, and four by the experts' group. The executive organ is the directorate, which is composed of three members.

c. *Financial Resources*

The resources are derived from contributions payable in equal parts by the insured persons and their employers, except in the case of insured persons who do not receive cash wages and for whom the employer is required to pay the whole contribution. Insured persons are divided into five wage classes, the weekly contribution for the different classes varying from 2.60 to 8.40 crowns.[6] The State pays a subsidy only to pensioners (i. e. persons entitled to one of the following pensions: invalidity, old-age, widows' and orphans'), which varies in accordance with the category to which the beneficiary belongs.

d. *Benefits*

The insurance scheme makes provision for invalidity pensions, old-age pensions, and widows' and orphans' pensions. In addition, dowries are granted to insured women who marry, and lump-sum payments are made to survivors of insured persons who die before acquiring the right to a pension. The right to a pension is subject to the payment of one hundred weekly contributions, including at least thirteen under compulsory insurance.

1. An invalidity pension is granted to an insured person who, as the result of sickness or infirmity not incurred intentionally, is incapable of earning, in employment suited to his strength, ability, training, and previous occupation, at least

one-third of the amount usually earned by workers of the same class with similar training.

The pension includes a basic amount of 550 crowns per year, plus an increment fixed in proportion to the number of weekly contributions paid by or on behalf of the insured person, and varying from 0.60 to 1.75 crowns (or about one-fifth of the insurance contributions paid), plus a supplement equal to one-tenth of the pension for each dependent child under seventeen years of age. When in the preceding year the income of a pensioner from other sources than his pension has not exceeded the minimum amount (7,000 crowns per year) exempted from income tax, the pensioner is entitled to a State subsidy of 500 crowns a year.

2. An old-age pension is granted to an insured person who has attained the age of sixty-five years and is no longer engaged in any work or service liable to insurance, or who earns from such work or service less than one-half of the amount usually earned by a worker in the same district with similar training in the same occupation. The old-age pension is assessed in the same way as the invalidity pension.

3. A widow's pension is granted to the widow of a pensioner at the age of sixty-five years or at an earlier age if she becomes incapacitated. A widow is entitled to a pension at an earlier age even if she is capable of working, provided that she maintains at least two children under seventeen years of age. An incapacitated widower who was mainly or wholly maintained by his wife is also entitled to a pension. A widow's or widower's pension amounts to one-half of the pension to which the insured person was entitled or would have been entitled at the time of his death. The State subsidy to the widow's or widower's pension amounts to 250 crowns a year. Invalidity, old-age, and widow's pensions may be increased by 50 per cent for persons who require the constant assistance of another.

4. An orphan's pension is granted to children under seventeen years of age of a deceased pensioner or an insured person

who has completed the qualifying period. The pension is equal to one-fifth of the pension of the deceased, but is increased to two-fifths in the case of children who have lost both parents. The State subsidy is 100 crowns a year, which is increased to 200 crowns a year for a child who has lost both parents.

5. There are several minor provisions of the act. Insured women who marry after completing the qualifying period of one hundred weeks are entitled to a dowry, which varies from 400 to 600 crowns according to the wage class to which they belong. Also, the survivors of an insured person who, at the time of his death, had not completed the qualifying period are entitled to a lump sum which varies from 550 to 750 crowns according to his wage class. In addition to cash benefits, the Central Institution grants treatment which may avert invalidity which might result from the sickness of the insured person, his wife, or his widow.

2. SALARIED EMPLOYEES' INSURANCE

a. *Scope*

Insurance is compulsory for:

1. all persons employed under a contract of employment or service on work of an essentially intellectual character;

2. salaried employees working in offices, with the exception of those engaged in cleaning, manifolding documents by purely mechanical processes, or on other work which cannot be deemed to be office work;

3. all persons employed in business houses on commercial work or on other work of a higher order, as well as all persons employed on non-commercial work in undertakings and establishments mentioned in the Act (undertakings coming under the Industrial Code, credit establishments, savings banks, publishers' offices, barristers' and notaries' offices, etc.);

4. persons entrusted with supervisory duties in undertakings of every sort, or responsible for storage of goods;

5. permanent representatives of undertakings of every description.

The insurance scheme does not apply to young persons under sixteen years of age or to persons whose employment in an occupation entailing liability to insurance is of a subsidiary nature. Salaried employees of the State, provinces, communes, and other bodies corporate are excluded from insurance when their service regulations guarantee them benefits at least equal to those provided under this Act.

b. *Administration*

The insurance system is administered by the General Pension Institution at Prague and by a number of so-called substitute institutions set up on the lines of establishment funds. All salaried employees who are not affiliated with a substitute institution automatically belong to the General Institution.

The main administrative organs of the General Institution are the board and the governing body, both of which comprise equal numbers of employee members and employer members, and also a number of social insurance experts appointed by the Government. The chairman of the institution is appointed by the Head of the State. The executive organ is the directorate of three members.

c. *Financial Resources*

The resources of the insurance scheme are derived from contributions which are payable in equal parts by salaried employees and their employers. The insured persons are divided into eleven salary classes, in accordance with their annual remuneration. The joint contribution of the employer and the employee varies from 12 to 250 crowns a month, according to salary class. The State does not contribute toward this insurance.

d. *Benefits*

The insurance system makes provision for the payment of invalidity pensions, old-age pensions, widows' pensions, orphans' pensions, and parents' pensions. Lump-sum payments are also granted to insured women in the event of marriage.

The right to a pension is conditional upon the completion of a qualifying period of sixty contribution months. Survivors of an insured person who dies before the completion of the necessary qualifying period receive a lump-sum payment instead of a pension.

1. An invalidity pension is granted to an insured person who, as a result of bodily or mental infirmity, or a decline in health, is no longer able to perform the duties of his occupation or of any other occupation suitable to his practical and theoretical training. The invalidity pension consists of a basic sum of 3,600 crowns a year, plus an increment based on the number of contribution months completed by the beneficiary, varying from 2 to 50 crowns according to his salary class. A children's bonus equal to one-eighth of the total pension including the increment is granted for each child under eighteen years of age maintained by the insured person.

2. An old-age pension is granted to insured men who have reached their sixtieth year and who have at least 480 contribution months to their credit, and to insured women who have completed their fifty-fifth year, provided they are not engaged in an occupation which is covered by insurance. The old-age pension is calculated in the same manner as the invalidity pension. The old-age pension (in this case styled "social pension") is also payable to insured men who have attained the age of fifty-six (women fifty-four) who have been in the compulsory insurance system for at least 120 months, and who have been unemployed for not less than one year.[7]

3. A widow's pension is granted to the widow of a pensioner or insured person who dies after completing the qualifying period. It is equal to one-half of the pension to which the deceased person was, or would have been, entitled, but may not be less than 3,000 crowns a year. A similar pension is granted to the widower of an insured woman who, at the time of her death, was in receipt of a pension, or would have been entitled to a pension, and who supported her husband out of her earnings. This pension is paid to the widower only if and

so long as he is incapable of work and in need. A widow who re-marries receives an indemnity equal to three times the widow's pension.

4. An orphan's pension is granted to each child of the deceased who is under eighteen years of age. It amounts to one-quarter of the pension of the deceased, with a minimum of 1,500 crowns a year. In the case of an orphan, both of whose parents are dead, the pension is fixed at one-half the deceased parent's pension subject to a minimum of 3000 crowns. The pension may be granted up to the age of twenty-four years if the child has not completed his vocational training or is unable to provide for himself owing to an infirmity. Grandchildren of the deceased person who were mainly dependent upon him for their maintenance are also entitled to a pension, provided that the aggregate amount of the widow's pension and that of the children does not exceed the pension of the deceased.

5. A parent's pension is granted to the parents of the deceased who were mainly dependent on him for their maintenance, provided he leaves neither widow nor children. It is equal to one-quarter of his pension, with a minimum of 1,500 crowns a year. If both parents are living, each of them receives one-eighth of his pension, with a minimum of 750 crowns a year.

6. An insured woman who marries after completing 60 contribution months is entitled to a dowry equal to the amount of the annual invalidity pension to which she would be entitled in her salary class, by virtue of contributions paid by her or on her behalf. In case of the death of an insured person who has completed at least six contribution months, but who has not completed the qualifying period, the widow and, in default of a widow, the children are entitled to an allowance amounting to one and one-half times the annual amount of invalidity pension which would have been payable to the deceased if he had completed 60 contribution months. In the case of surviving parents, this allowance is equal to one-half of that which would be payable to the widow or orphans of the deceased.

Funeral benefit equal to one-fifth of the pension of the deceased person, but not in any case more than 4,000 crowns, is paid to the near relatives of the deceased who defray the cost of burial. In addition to cash benefits, medical treatment and care may be granted to insured persons and pensioners with a view to averting or curing invalidity.

3. MINERS' INSURANCE

a. *Scope*

Insurance is compulsory for all persons employed in Czechoslovakia in mining undertakings, irrespective of age, sex, or nationality.

b. *Administration*

The insurance scheme is administered by the Central Miners' Benefit Society in Prague. The local organs of the Central Society are the district benefit societies responsible for the administration of sickness insurance, of which there are eight, one for the area of each district mining authority. The executive organs of the Central Society are the general assembly, the governing body, and the supervising committee. These bodies are composed of representatives elected by the insured persons and their employers.

c. *Financial Resources*

The resources are derived from contributions, which are fixed for all insured persons, irrespective of salary, at 87 crowns a month, of which 33 crowns are paid by the insured person and 54 crowns by the employer. In addition to the regular contribution of 87 crowns a month, the Act of July 3, 1936 provided for a number of emergency contributions for an initial ten-year period ending in 1946. The employer is required to pay the whole contribution for persons not in receipt of cash wages, or who receive only a small wage because their occupational training is not complete.

c. *Benefits*

Benefits include invalidity pensions, old-age pensions, and widows' and orphans' pensions.

1. An invalidity pension is paid to an insured person who becomes incapable of carrying on his occupation. It may be claimed by an underground worker who has lost at least 40 per cent of his working capacity, and by a surface worker who has lost 50 per cent of his working capacity. The right to a pension is acquired after the completion of a qualifying period of two years. If the circumstances justifying the payment of a pension occur prior to the completion of the qualifying peroid, but after at least three years' affiliation, the insured person is entitled to claim a pension equal to two-thirds of the full pension. No qualifying period is required when invalidity results from an industrial accident.

The pension comprises a basic sum of 300 crowns a year plus an increment at the rate of 7.50 crowns for each contribution month after the completion of the qualifying period, and a State subsidy of 500 crowns per year. The pension of an incapacitated person whose condition entails the constant help of another person is increased by one-half.

2. An old-age pension is payable after 360 contribution months to insured persons who have reached the age of fifty-five and are no longer employed as miners. Insured persons who have paid 180 monthly contributions may claim a pension at the age of sixty. The old-age pension is calculated in the same way as the invalidity pension.

3. A widow's pension is granted to the widow of a pensioner or insured person who dies after having completed the qualifying period. There is no age-limit for the widow. The pension is equal to one-half of the pension to which the deceased person was or would have been entitled. In case of remarriage, the widow's pension is commuted by the payment of a lump sum equal to three times her annual pension. The State pays a supplement of 250 crowns a year.

4. An orphan's pension is payable to each child of a deceased pensioner or insured person up to the age of sixteen years, and without any age limit in the case of children who are totally incapable of earning their living because of mental or physical infirmity. The orphan's pension is equal to one-fifth of the pension to which the deceased was or would have been entitled in case of invalidity. An orphan who has lost both parents is entitled to two-fifths the deceased person's pension. The pensions of the widow and children together may not exceed three-quarters of the pension to which the deceased was or would have been entitled. The State pays a supplement of 100 crowns a year.

4. NON-CONTRIBUTORY OLD-AGE PENSIONS

a. *Scope*

The Act of March 21, 1929,[8] introduced a system of non-contributory pensions for persons who, on July 1, 1926, when the general scheme of invalidity, old-age, and widows' and orphans' pensions went into force, were too old to enter into insurance. By this act, all persons in indigent circumstances and incapable of work who do not come within the scope of the Act of October 9, 1924, because they were over sixty years of age at the time when that act went into force are entitled to a pension upon reaching their sixty-fifth year. As a rule, pensions are reserved for citizens of Czechoslovakia. However, they may be granted to aliens when their country extends the benefit of its non-contributory pension system to Czechoslovak nationals.

b. *Administration*

The pension system is administered by the communal and district authorities. Pension claims must be made to the commune in which the claimant lives, the final decision being made by the administrative authority of the district to which the commune belongs.

c. *Financial Resources*

The cost of pensions is borne by the State. The commune in which the beneficiary resides is required to pay a supplementary allowance, which varies with the number of inhabitants in the commune. The rate is fixed at 10 per cent of the State pension in communes with a population not exceeding 2,000, at 15 per cent in communes with a population of 2,000 to 50,000, and at 20 per cent in communes with a population of over 50,000.

d. *Benefits*

The pension payable by the State amounts to 500 crowns per year. To this sum is added the supplementary allowance granted by the commune. When two persons living in the same household become entitled to a pension, the pension of each is reduced to 300 crowns per year, except when one of the pensioners requires the constant help of another person. The pension payable by the State is reduced by the amount of any other assistance benefit to which the pensioner is entitled by law.

5. COMPARISON OF INVALIDITY, OLD-AGE, WIDOWS' AND ORPHANS' INSURANCE AND PENSION LEGISLATION OF CZECHOSLOVAKIA WITH I.L.O. STANDARDS

At the seventeenth session of the International Labor Conference in Geneva in 1933, six Conventions concerning invalidity, old-age, and widows' and orphans' pensions in industrial and agricultural undertakings were adopted. None of these Conventions have been ratified by Czechoslovakia, although in each case the legislation of Czechoslovakia compares favorably with the standards set up by the Conventions. The Conventions regarding invalidity insurance, on the one hand, apply to manual and non-manual workers, including apprentices employed in industrial or commercial undertakings or in the liberal professions, and to out-workers and domestic servants, and on the other hand, to manual and non-manual workers, including apprentices, employed in agricultural undertakings, and domestic servants employed in the households of agricultural employers. All of these groups are included in Czech legislation.

The Conventions state that an insured person who becomes incapacitated for work shall be entitled to an invalidity pension upon the completion of a qualifying period which shall not exceed sixty contribution months, two hundred and fifty contribution weeks, or fifteen hundred contribution days. Czechoslovak legislation provides a qualifying period of one hundred contribution weeks for workers; sixty contribution months for salaried employees; five contribution years for miners. The Conventions state that the pension shall be a fixed sum or a percentage of the remuneration taken into account for insurance purposes, or vary with the amount of the contributions paid. The legislation of Czechoslovakia provides for the payment of a basic amount plus an increment fixed in proportion to the number of weekly or monthly contributions paid by the insured person.

The Conventions further provide that the insured persons and their employers shall contribute to the financial resources of the insurance scheme. In Czechoslovakia, the resources for workers' and salaried employees' insurance are derived from contributions payable in equal parts by the insured persons and their employers, while the resources for miners' insurance are derived from contributions which are fixed for all insured persons, irrespective of salary, at 87 crowns a month, of which 33 crowns are paid by the insured person and 54 crowns by the employer. The Conventions also state that the insurance scheme shall be administered by institutions founded by the public authorities and not conducted with a view to profit, or by State insurance funds. In Czechoslovakia, the workers' insurance scheme is administered by the Central Social Insurance Institution at Prague, the salaried employees' scheme is administered by the General Pension Institution at Prague, and the miners' insurance scheme is administered by the Central Miners' Benefit Society in Prague, all of which are under State supervision and are not run for profit.

The Conventions concerning compulsory old-age insurance apply to persons employed in industrial or commercial undertakings, in the liberal professions, and to out-workers and domestic servants, on the one hand, and on the other, to persons employed in agricultural undertakings. All these groups are covered by the legislation of Czechoslovakia. The Conventions state that an insured person shall be entitled to an old-age pension at an age which shall not exceed sixty-five, and that the pension shall be a fixed sum, or a percentage of the remuneration taken into account for insurance purposes, or vary with the amount of the contributions paid. In Czechoslovakia, old-age pensions are paid to insured workers and salaried employees at sixty-five years of age, and to miners at fifty-five years of age. In each of the three schemes, the old-age pensions are assessed in the same way as the invalidity pensions, both the insured persons and the employers contributing to the insurance resources. This is also in accord with the Conventions, which state that the insured persons and their employers shall contribute to the financial resources of the insurance scheme.

The same similarities may be found between the Conventions concerning compulsory widows' and orphans' insurance for persons employed in industrial and in agricultural undertakings. The Conventions state that the right to a widow's pension may be reserved to widows who are above a prescribed age or who are invalids. Any child who has not reached a prescribed age, which shall not be less than fourteen, shall be entitled to a pension in respect of the death of either parent. They further provide that the pension shall, whether or not dependent on the time spent in insurance, be a fixed sum or a percentage of the remuneration taken into account for insurance purposes, or vary with the amount of the contributions paid.

In the workers' insurance scheme in Czechoslovakia, a widow's pension is granted to the widow of a pensioner at the age of sixty-five years, or at an earlier age if she becomes incapacitated. In the salaried employees' and miners' schemes, a pension is granted to the widow of a pensioner or insured person who dies after completing the qualifying period. There is no age requirement in the latter two schemes.

In the workers' scheme, an orphan's pension is granted to children under seventeen years of age, in the salaried employees' scheme to children under eighteen years of age, and in the miners' scheme to children under sixteen generally, and to all children, regardless of age, who are totally incapable of earning their living because of mental or physical infirmity. In the workers' scheme, the orphan's pension is equal to one-fifth of the pension of the deceased person, and in the salaried employees' and miners' schemes, the pension is equal to one-quarter of the pension of the deceased person.[9]

---

1 *Bulletin of International Labor Office*, Basle, Switzerland, I [1907], 398.

2 Austrian crown = 20.3 cents.

3 *Legislative Series*, 1924, Cz. 4; 1928, Cz. 2; 1934, Cz.4.

4 *Ibid.*, 1929, Cz. 1; 1931, Cz. 2; 1934, Cz. 5.

5 *Ibid.*, 1922, Cz. 2; 1934, Cz. 5; I. L. O. Year-Book 1935-1936, p. 230; 1936-1937, p. 234.

6 In 1922, exchange rate of crown was stabilized at 100 crowns to $3.00.—(*Encyclopaedia Britannica*, 14th ed.; VI, 954.) In the second quarter of 1938, on the N. Y. Exchange, 100 crowns were quoted at $3.48⅛.

7 *Legislative Series*, 1934, Cz. 5, p. 538.

8 *International Survey of Social Services*, 1933 (International Labor Office, Geneva, Switzerland, 1936), p. 144.

9 For the texts of the Conventions concerning invalidity, old-age, and widows' and orphans' insurance for persons employed in industrial or commercial undertakings, in the liberal professions, and for out-workers and domestic servants, and for persons employed in agricultural undertakings, see *Official Bulletin*, XVIII, 306-365.

CHAPTER VI

(1) WORKMEN'S COMPENSATION

A. In Austria Prior to 1918

In 1887, the compulsory Accident Insurance Law was enacted, followed in 1888 by the passing of the compulsory Sickness Insurance Law.[1]

1. SCOPE

The Accident Insurance Law of 1887 applied to industries conducted on a large scale, and to industries in which there was a high accident rate, such as those involving the use of explosives or of power-driven machinery. The law also included those workmen in agriculture and forestry who were exposed to the risk of machinery. The Law of 1894 extended the insurance to the transportation industries, to warehousing and storage industries, and the cleaning of streets. The existing miners' provident funds were not affected by either the 1887 or 1894 Accident Insurance Laws, so that the insurance of miners was entirely separate from the insurance of other workers.

The Sickness Insurance Law of 1888 specified that all persons included in the accident insurance law were subject to the compulsory sickness insurance. By this provision, the first four weeks of disability caused by accident were cared for in all the industries included in the accident insurance.

The persons insured were workmen and administrative officials employed in factories and smelting works, in mining operations on non-reserved minerals, in shipyards, in slips, and in quarries, as well as in plants connected with these establishments; in building operations; in establishments producing or using explosives; in establishments engaged in manufacturing and in industries generally; in agriculture or forestry in which steam boilers were used or machinery moved by animal or mechanical power.

In addition, the Law of 1894 placed the following establishments under the insurance system: all parts of the operation of railways, regardless of the motive power used; all other transportation enterprises (not including navigation, which was covered by the maritime code) which conducted as a business the transportation of persons or commodities either on land or on rivers and inland waterways; dredging operations; establishments for cleaning streets and buildings; establishments conducting storage houses, including warehouses, lumber yards, coal yards, etc.; paid fire departments or services, establishments for digging canals; establishments for cleaning chimneys; establishments for stone-cutting, well-digging, and construction work in iron and steel, including establishments not before covered by the insurance system.

The law included in the insurance both workmen and administrative officials. There was no specified limit as to the wages or salary received by these persons. The terms also included apprentices, learners, workers without pay, etc., who because of unfinished training received either no wages or reduced wages. Heads of establishments not included under the law might voluntarily insure themselves and their employees. Also, in establishments covered by the law, those persons not included in the terms workmen and administrative officials might be insured in the same way as those covered by the law. The earnings of such persons in excess of 1,200 florins ($487.20) were not considered in computing premiums and compensation. Persons who were members of volunteer fire departments or services might also insure themselves on the same terms as paid departments.

The accidents compensated were those occurring during the employment. The accident must have a direct connection with the employment or, as the law designated it, there must be a "causal connection" between the accident and the employment. Accidents caused purposely were the only class of accidents not compensated, but these were granted compensation if the injury terminated in death. No other benefits than those prescribed in the law might be granted, so that disability due to invalidity or diseases caused by special occupations or dangerous trades was not regarded as coming within the scope of the law.

2. ADMINISTRATION

The administrative head of the accident insurance, as well as of the sickness insurance, was the Minister of the Interior, who was entrusted with the enforcement of the laws and with issuing the decrees authorized by the laws. Connected with the Ministry of the Interior was the insurance council, whose functions were advisory rather than executive. Under the Minister of the Interior, the organizations known as insurance institutions performed the actual work of accident insurance. The law required that an insurance institution be organized by the employers, workmen, and administrative officials of the establishments covered by the law and that such an association be organized for each of the principal geographical divisions of the country.

3. FINANCIAL RESOURCES

The means for defraying the cost of the accident insurance were obtained from assessments based on the pay roll of each establishment, modified by a system of risk ratings. The employer was required to forward to the institution the entire amount of the insurance assessments, but was authorized to deduct 10 per cent of the assessments from the wages of his insured employees. The system in use in Austria, where the sick funds provided for the first four weeks of all cases of disability, of which the employer paid one-third, was responsible for the plan of having the workmen pay one-tenth of the cost of the accident insurance. The State made no direct payments to the insurance system, but provided the services of a large number of officials (such as judicial officials for the arbitration of controversies) and gave the services of the money-order system of the Post-Office Department for the payment of the pensions.

4. BENEFITS

a. *Medical Attendance*

The accident insurance organizations were institutions which provided financial benefits only. Medicines, medical attendance, therapeutic appliances, etc., in case of accidental injury must be provided, as long as the disability lasted, by the sickness insurance organization. To carry out this provision, the sick funds in the area of each accident insurance institution were organized into a federation, and the work of providing the medical benefits was performed by the federation. The accident institution administered the business of the federation.

b. *Pensions for Disability*

In case of disability due to accident, the sickness insurance organizations must provide the benefits specified under the sickness insurance law for the first four weeks of disability. The accident insurance institutions must provide pensions beginning with the fifth week of disability.

The pension was computed on the basis of the average annual earnings of the injured person, or of a person engaged in similar work in the same or a similar establishment. The average annual earnings were computed at 300 times the average daily earnings, but if the annual earnings exceeded 1,200 florins ($487.20), the excess was not considered in computing the pension.

The pension for total disability was equal in amount to 60 percent of the annual earnings. For partial disability the pension was a portion of the preceding, depending on the loss of earning power, but not to exceed 50 per cent of the annual earnings. Pensions might, with the consent of the pensioner and the approval of certain officials of the commune in which he resided, be paid off wholly or partly on the basis of the capitalized value of the pension. Pensions to persons residing permanently in foreign countries might be paid off by such payments.

In order to place the employees of railways in as favorable position as they were under the Liability Law of 1869, the Insurance Law of 1894 contained a special provision that railway employees were to have their fund earnings counted in computing the assessments and the compensation. Also the assessments were paid entirely by the employer, instead of 90 per cent by the employer and 10 per cent by the workman. The compensation was made larger in certain cases by the provision that if the injured railway employee or his dependent heirs had a claim under the Liability Law of 1869, the accident pension specified for other industries should be increased one-half for temporary disability and should be doubled for complete permanent disability.

c. *Funeral Benefits*

The funeral benefit consisted of the expense of burial, with a maximum of 25 florins ($10.15).

d. *Pensions to Survivors*

If the injured person died as the result of the accident, pensions must be paid to the survivors. These pensions were as follows:

(1) to the widow, 20 per cent of the annual earnings of the deceased until her death or remarriage, and in the latter case, a lump sum equal to three annual payments as a settlement;

(2) to each legitimate child until the completion of the fifteenth year of age, 15 per cent, and if such child lost the other parent, 20 per cent;

(3) to each illegitimate child during the same age period, 10 per cent.

The pensions to the widow and children together might not exceed 50 per cent of the annual earnings of the deceased. In case the dependents already mentioned did not exhaust the 50 per cent, the parents or grandparents of the deceased, if they were solely supported by him, might receive a pension of not more than 20 per cent. This pension continued during life or while dependent.

B. In Hungary Prior to 1918

Act No. 14 of 1891, as amended by Act No. 19 of 1907, provided for compulsory insurance against accidents in the case of the following undertakings and occupations:

1. Mines, foundries, salt works, and other works for working up mining products; quarries, sand pits, gravel pits, and clay pits, and undertakings for the breaking and working up of stone and earth;

2. The construction of roads, bridges, tunnels, water-works, dams, canals, harbors, fortifications, system for the transmission of water, gas, electric light and power;

3. Establishments in which inflammable, noxious, or poisonous materials, or explosives are manufactured or prepared;

4. Chemical, physical, and pharmaceutical laboratories;

5. Slaughter houses, meat trade, sausage works, ice factories;

6. Railways, irrespective of the motive power used, factories, and workshops, and construction and maintenance works connected therewith; post, telegraph, and telephone undertakings, and the construction and maintenance of them;

7. Shipping, including ships' restaurants; loading and shipbuilding;

8. Dredging and harbor works, ferries, and rafting;

9. Carrying and forwarding of goods; warehouses, and commercial stores;

10. Industries subsidiary to agriculture, forestry, stockbreaking, fishery, horticulture, viticulture, sericulture, and beekeeping;

11. Public institutions;

12. State, municipal, communal, and institutional undertakings, except military works and undertakings employing soldiers;

13. Workshops attached to public educational institutions;

14. Unions, societies, industrial corporations, and the insurance funds set up in accordance with this act;

15. Domestic service;

16. The work of certified engineers in charge of agricultural work;

17. All building undertakings and workyards, including construction undertaken not commercially, but by or on behalf of a public authority, unless such construction does not require a building permit;

18. Professional fire brigades;

19. Motor-car driving;

20. Undertakings in which persons in reformatories or prisons are employed.

All benefits and the cost of treatment for the first ten weeks were provided by the sick funds to which employers and employees contributed equally. Beginning with the eleventh week, the entire cost was defrayed by the employer, through the accident fund.

In case of death, a funeral benefit of 20 times the average daily wage was paid. Pensions to heirs, not exceeding 60 per cent of the annual earnings of the deceased, were paid as follows:

(a) to the widow, 20 per cent of the annual earnings, until death or remarriage; in the latter case, a final sum equal to 60 per cent of annual earnings; to a dependent widower, 20 per cent during disability;

(b) to each child sixteen years of age or under, 15 per cent if one parent survived, 30 per cent is neither survived; payments to widow and children were reduced proportionately if they aggregated more than 60 per cent;

(c) to dependent parents and grandparents, 20 per cent or less, if there was a residue after providing for the other heirs;

(d) to dependent orphan grandchildren, fifteen years of age or under, 20 per cent or less if there was a residue after providing for the other heirs.

Where both parties were insured and both died as the result of an accident, the pension was based on the earnings of the one receiving the highest wages. Pensions were allowed after a child had completed his sixteenth year if necessary to enable him to complete his education. In computing pensions, the excess of annual earnings above 2,400 crowns ($487.20) was not considered.

In case of disability, the following benefits were paid:

(a) free medical and surgical treatment provided for the first ten weeks by the sickness fund and afterward by the accident fund;

(b) for temporary or permanent total disability, 50 per cent of the average daily wages, but not exceeding 4 crowns (81 cents) for the first ten weeks, provided by the sickness fund; beginning with the eleventh week, 60 per cent of the average annual earnings, provided by the accident fund;

(c) for complete helplessness, necessitating attendance, payments might be increased to 100 per cent of the annual earnings;

(d) for partial disability, a corresponding portion of full pension;

(e) in computing pensions, the excess of annual earnings above 2,400 crowns was not considered.

The Act of 1900 provided for compulsory insurance against accidents in water-works companies, and in the water-works and forestry undertakings under the Ministry of Agriculture. The Act of June 26, 1902, was amended by the Act of July 3, 1909, on relief funds for agricultural workers and farm servants, the Act of February 27, 1912, on the insurance of agricultural workers and farm servants against industrial accidents, and the Act of June 28, 1913, on the insurance of agricultural workers against sickness and accident, set up a relief fund which, since the Act of 1913, has been called the "Relief Fund for Agricultural Workers." [2]

C. In Czechoslovakia

I. WORKMEN'S COMPENSATION FOR INDUSTRIAL ACCIDENTS

a. *In Bohemia, Moravia, and Silesia*

Compulsory insurance against industrial accidents in Bohemia, Moravia, and Silesia is governed by the old Austrian Act of December 28, 1887, as amended by the old Austrian Act of July 20, 1894, and by the Czechoslovak laws of April 10, 1919, and August 12, 1921.[3]

1. Scope

Insurance is compulsory, irrespective of age, sex, and nationality, for workers and apprentices employed in:

(a) factories, iron works, foundries, mineral mines not worked under concession, workyards, quarries, smelting of ores under concession, and undertakings for the production of mineral wax and asphalt;

(b) industrial undertakings carrying out building operations and works connected with house-building;

(c) industrial agricultural and forestry undertakings, using boilers or machines worked by natural or animal power;

(d) industrial undertakings manufacturing or using explosive materials;

(e) undertakings engaged in the transport of persons and goods by land, river, or sea;

(f) dredging operations;

(g) industrial undertakings engaged in the cleaning of streets and buildings, canals, and chimneys;

(h) industrial undertakings for cellarage and storage, and wood and coal depots;

(i) permanent theatrical undertakings;

(j) industrial undertakings engaged in stone-cutting and metal forging.

The following undertakings are excluded from the scope of insurance:

(a) undertakings temporarily employing machinery not forming part of their plant;

(b) the construction of dwelling houses and agricultural buildings in rural areas, provided that only the builder, the members of his family, and other persons living in the same commune, who are themselves not builders by trade, are employed on such work.

2. Administration

The insurance scheme is administered by two territorial institutions, one with headquarters at Prague, the other at Brno. The managing committee of each institution is composed of equal numbers of employers' representatives, insured persons' representatives, and persons acquainted with the economic situation of the district, appointed by the Minister of Social Welfare. These institutions are subject to State supervision.

3. Financial Resources

The money required to cover the cost of benefits, administrative expenses, and the accumulation of a reserve fund is derived from contributions payable by the employers. The scheme is based on the annual assessment of the capital value of pensions. The contribution of each employer is fixed according to the coefficient of risk of each class of undertaking and the aggregate wages earned by the insured workers. In assessing contributions, no account is taken of wages in excess of 12,000 crowns per year per worker.

4. Benefits

Insurance covers accidents occurring in the undertaking or establishment, as well as accidents due to the performance of domestic or other work outside the insured occupation, when such work is carried out at the employer's orders or on his behalf. Insurance also covers accidents occurring to workers between their home and their place of work, provided that the insured person has not stopped on the way for his own personal affairs, or for other reasons having no connection with his work.

(a) *Benefits in kind*

Victims of accidents are entitled to medical treatment and drugs. These benefits are provided by the sickness insurance scheme, the cost being borne by accident insurance as from the fifth week following the accident.

(c) *Benefits in case of incapacity*

(1) In case of total incapacity for work, the insured person is entitled to a pension equal to two-thirds of his annual wage. This wage is calculated by multiplying the average daily earnings during the year by 300. No account is taken of any wages in excess of 12,000 crowns per year. The maximum insurable wage for apprentices varies from a minimum of 2,250 crowns to a maximum of 5,400 crowns. If the victim of an accident requires the constant help of another persons, the pension may be increased by 50 per cent.

(2) In case of partial incapacity for work, the pension is fixed at a fraction of the total pension, corresponding to the loss of working capacity.

(d) *Benefits in case of death*

Survivors' pensions are paid to the widow, children, and other near relatives of the deceased, as follows:

(1) the pension of the widow (or incapacitated widower) amounts to 20 per cent of the basic wage of the deceased. In case of remarriage, the widow's pension is commuted for a lump sum equal to three times the annual pension;

(2) each child under fifteen years of age, left by the deceased, is entitled to a pension of 15 per cent of his wage, and orphans bereft of both parents, to a pension of 20 per cent. The pension is payable after fifteen years of age to children who, as a result of physical or mental infirmity, are entirely incapable of supporting themselves;

(3) the combined pensions of the widow and children may not exceed two-thirds of the annual wages of the deceased;

(4) when the combined widow's and orphan's pensions do not reach this maximum, relatives in the ascending line, grandchildren, brothers, and sisters, who were mainly dependent on the deceased, are entitled to a pension not exceeding 20 per cent of the basic wage;

(5) in addition to the pension, an allowance for funeral expenses not exceeding 900 crowns is granted on the death of an insured person.

b. *In Slovakia and Carpathian Ruthenia*

Compulsory insurance is governed by the old Hungarian Act No. XIX of 1907, as amended by the Orders of September 23, 1919, and July 14, 1922.[4]

1. Scope

Insurance is compulsory, irrespective of age, sex, and nationality, for workers and apprentices employed in:

(a) mines, factories, salt works, and other industries working up the products of mines, stone and sand quarries, gravel and clay pits, and undertakings, establishments, and works where stone or earth is broken up or transformed;

(b) the construction of roads, bridges, railways, tunnels, water-works, dams, canals, harbors, fortifications, and systems for the transmission of water, gas, and electric light and power;

(c) establishments in which inflammable, noxious, or poisonous substances, or explosive materials, or explosives are produced or handled;

(d) chemical, physical, and pharmaceutical laboratories;

(e) slaughter-houses, butchers', and pork butchers' establishments, and ice-factories;

(f) railways, whatever the motive power employed, and factories and workshops, and construction or repair maintenance work connected therewith, as well as the postal, telegraph, and telephone services;

(g) inland navigation and the loading of ships;

(h) dredging undertakings, work in harbors, on waterways, and all floating operations;

(i) undertakings engaged in the forwarding, handling, and storage of goods;

(j) all establishments subsidiary to agriculture, forestry, stock-breeding, and fishing;

(k) public undertakings and establishments and work for the State, municipalities, and communes;

(l) unions, companies, and industrial cooperative societies;

(m) domestic service;

(n) all building undertakings and work yards;

(o) undertakings employing persons detained in reformatories or prisons;

(p) the driving of motor vehicles.

2. Administration

The insurance scheme is administered by the Workers' Insurance Institute at Bratislava. The managing committee of the Institute is composed of nine employers' representatives and nine representatives of the insured persons.

3. Financial Resources

The financial resources are obtained in the same way as in Bohemia, Moravia, and Silesia.

4. Benefits

Insurance covers accidents occurring during the performance of work ordered by the employer or his representative, or in the interests of the undertaking.

With the exception of certain small details, cash benefits and benefits in kind are, on the whole, similar to those provided for in Bohemia, Moravia, and Silesia. Orphans' pensions are, however, paid up to the age of sixteen years.

c. *Special Scheme for Agricultural Workers*

The special scheme for agricultural workers is governed by the old Hungarian Acts No. II of 1898 and No. XVI of 1900, as amended by the old Hungarian Acts Nos. XIV of 1904, VIII of 1912, XX of 1913, and by the Czechoslovak Orders of August 23, 1919, and July 24, 1920.[5]

1. Scope

The insurance fund for agricultural workers at Bratislava includes foundation members, ordinary members, and affiliated members. Any person who pays a lump sum of at least 500 crowns is deemed to be a foundation member. Ordinary members are divided into five groups. Groups I and II comprise all agricultural laborers, farm servants, and other classes of agricultural workers who were between fourteen and thirty-five years of age at the time of joining the fund. Group III includes all persons who make provision for the payment of funeral expenses to their family in case of their death; Group IV, persons who insure for the payment of an allowance at a certain age, and Group V, all persons, wage earners or others, whose main occupation is agricultural work. Every agricultural worker may acquire the status of affiliated member by joining the insurance fund for agricultural workers. All agricultural workers and farm servants, whether using agricultural machinery or not, are liable to compulsory insurance. The employer is deemed to have satisfied the requirements of the Act by registering his workers and servants as affiliated members of the fund.

2. Administration

The insurance scheme is administered by the Agricultural Workers' Insurance Fund in Bratislava. The management of the Fund includes the chairman, four members elected by the general meeting, four members elected by the local committees, and four members appointed by the Minister of Agriculture. The Fund is under state supervision. A local committee is set up in each commune in which the Fund has at least forty members.

3. Financial Resources

Insurance is based on the accumulative system. The income of the Fund is derived from employers' contributions, contributions from voluntary members, a State subsidy, and gifts. The employer is required to make an annual lump-sum payment of 15 crowns for each worker and farm servant in his employment. The annual contributions of ordinary members vary according to their group, and amount to 104 crowns in Group I, 52 in Group II, 26 in Group III, 52 in Group IV, and 100 in Group V. The State contribution amounts to 150,000 crowns per year.

4. Benefits

Insurance covers accidents occurring during the perform of work, and resulting in incapacity for work, or death.

(a) *Benefits in case of incapacity*

(1) If the victim of an accident is incapable of earning one-half of the wage of an agricultural worker over a period exceeding one week, he is entitled to a daily allowance of 5 crowns for a maximum period of ten weeks. If the accident occurs during work, the employer is required to provide the victim with medical treatment, and to pay him a daily allowance of 5 crowns during a maximum period of ten weeks. Farm servants continue to receive their wages in all cases, and are entitled to board and lodging, the obligation of the Fund beginning only from the fifteenth week following the accident.

(2) If incapacity for work lasts for more than sixty days, the victim is entitled, as from the beginning of the eleventh week, to a pension equal to 2,400 crowns a year. When a loss of earning capacity of at least 25 per cent continues after the first ten weeks following the accident, the victim is entitled to a fraction of the total pension corresponding to his loss of earning capacity.

(b) *Benefits in case of death*

The family of the deceased is entitled to a lump-sum payment of 3,000 crowns. If he leaves more than two children under fourteen years of age, the allowance is increased by 500 crowns a year for each child up to a maximum of 5,000.

Members who have been affiliated with the fund for ten years and who, as a result of invalidity (even when not attributable to an occupational accident) are no longer able to earn one-half of the annual wages normally earned by agricultural workers of their locality, are entitled throughout the period of invalidity, to a pension of 100 crowns a year. Members who have reached the age of sixty-five years and are not in receipt of an invalidity pension, are entitled to a lump-sum payment of 500 crowns. On the death of a member who has been affiliated with the fund for at least five years, a lump-sum payment of 1,000 crowns is made to his family. If he has been affiliated for ten years, this allowance is increased to 1,250 crowns, and if affiliation has lasted fifteen years, to 1,500 crowns. If the deceased worker leaves more than three children, the widow is entitled to a special increment.

2. Equality of Treatment for National and Foreign Workers as Regards Workmen's Compensation for Accidents

Equality of treatment for national and foreign workers as regards workmen's compensation for accidents, is guaranteed by Czechoslovak legislation. The basic principles are laid down in the Act of December 28, 1887, respecting workers' accident insurance applicable to Bohemia, Moravia, and Silesia; Legislative Article No. XVI of 1900 respecting accident insurance for agricultural workers and servants, for the territories of Slovakia and Sub-Carpathian Russia; and Legislative Article No. XIX of 1907 respecting accident and sickness insurance for workers in industry and commerce in Slovakia and Sub-Carpathian Russia. Equality of treatment is not conditioned upon the foreign workers' permanent residence in Czechoslovak territory, so a foreign worker entitled to a pension does not forfeit his right to a pension for injury from accident by leaving Czechoslovak territory. In such cases, however, the insurance institutions are permitted to substitute for the pension the payment of a lump-sum in final settlement.

As regards the territories of Slovakia and Sub-Carpathian Russia, Legislative Article No. XIX of 1907 provides that if the person entitled to a pension is a foreign worker who returns to his country to reside there permanently, his pension for injury from accident continues to be paid, provided that the State in question observes reciprocity as regards Czechoslovak nationals. Relatives of foreign workers insured under the provisions of this Act and deceased as the result of an accident, who at the date of the accident are living abroad permanently, are entitled to compensation only if the State in question follows the same procedure with respect to dependents residing in Czechoslovakia, of Czechoslovak nationals who are insured persons and who die in that foreign country. If the dependents of a foreign worker who is already in receipt of a pension leave to make their permanent residence in a foreign country, they are entitled to a payment of three times the amount of the annual pension. If they return to Czechoslovakia, they have no further right to a pension. The question of reciprocity also applies to foreign dependents. The substitution of a lump-sum payment for the pension due to a foreign worker who has left the country, occurs very rarely, and only at the request of the pensioner. As a rule, the pension continues to be paid.

Equality of treatment has been arranged, up to the present, by an exchange of diplomatic notes between Czechoslovakia and Sweden, Finland, the Netherlands, France, Japan, Estonia, and Switzerland. A similar procedure is at present being followed between Czechoslovakia and Belgium, Hungary, Spain, Norway, Portugal, the Irish Free State, Bulgaria, and Cuba.

The payment of accident compensation has been arranged by treaty with Austria, Argentina, Germany, and Yugoslavia.

The documents in which the Austrian and Czechoslovak Republics ratified the Social Insurance Treaty signed in Prague in 1931 were exchanged on April 27, 1933.[6] The contracting States determined exactly the scope of their social insurance legislation and each agreed to accord equality of treatment to the nationals of the other. It was further provided that insured persons and pensioners who move from one country to the other shall keep their rights, and arrangements for mutual administrative and judicial assistance in respect of social insurance have also been made. The treaty covers insurance against sickness and maternity, industrial accidents, insurance of salaried employees against invalidity, old-age, and death, and miners' insurance. It does not cover invalidity, old-age, and widows' and orphans' insurance for workers, which is in normal operation only in Czechoslovakia.

In order to avoid gaps and overlapping, Austria and Czechoslovakia have defined exactly the scope of their social insurance schemes. First, the treaty confirms the principle that the insurance of an employed person is governed by the legislation in force at the place of work. Exceptions are made, however, in the interests of continuity of insurance, with regard to workers employed now in one country and now in the other. Persons sent by an undertaking situated in one country to work for a period not exceeding a year in the other remain under the legislation in force at the headquarters of the undertaking. The same applied to persons whose duties entail their being sent by an undertaking in one country to reside for repeated periods (not exceeding a year each) in the other, and to the employees of public transport undertakings who are employed provisionally or, in the case of service on communicating lines or in frontier stations, permanently on the territory of the other country. The object of all these exceptions is the same, namely, to establish the validity of the legislation in force at the headquarters of the undertaking to which the insured worker belongs.

Austrian and Czechoslovak legislation does not in theory make any distinction between national and foreign workers in respect of admission to the insurance systems, amount of contributions, and right to benefit. This freely granted equality is transformed by the treaty, as far as the nationals of the two contracting States are concerned, into a strict obligation. As regards industrial accidents, such an obligation already existed, since both Austria and Czechoslovakia had already ratified the International Labor Convention adopted at Geneva in 1925, concerning the equality of treatment for national and foreign workers as regards compensation for accidents.

On March 31, 1932, representatives of the Argentine and Czechoslovak Governments signed, at Buenos Aires, a treaty establishing equality of treatment as regards compensation for industrial accidents. An exchange of ratifications took place on November 9, 1934, and the treaty came into force on December 8, 1934. The two countries undertook to grant equality of treatment to each other's nationals as regards workers' compensation for accidents. No exceptions should be made to this rule, whatever changes took place in the domicile of the victim or his dependents in the two countries.

The Argentine and Czechoslovak Republics undertook to help each other mutually to facilitate the enforcement of their respective legislation, with special reference to the notification to be given to the dependents of the victim. The right to compensation should be regulated by the legislation of the country in which the accident occurred.

The treaty was to be valid for a period of five years, and would be deemed to be prolonged until terminated by a year's notice.[7]

The instruments of ratification of a treaty between Czechoslovakia and Germany relating to social insurance, which was signed at Berlin in 1931, were exchanged on November 16, 1933, and the treaty went into force on December 1, 1933.[8]

On December 14, 1936, a Social Insurance treaty was concluded between Czechoslovakia and Yugoslavia.[9] The provisions of these two treaties were similar to those of the treaties with Austria and Argentina.

3. Workmen's Compensation for Occupational Diseases

The Act of June 1, 1932,[10] provided that the provisions of the Act of December 28, 1887, respecting workers' accident insurance, of Act no. XIX of 1907 respecting sickness and accident insurance for persons employed in industry and commerce, of Act No. XVI of 1900 respecting the relief fund for agricultural laborers and servants (in so far as these Acts govern accident insurance), and the provisions of the legislative measures to supplement and amend these Acts, shall apply to occupational diseases.

By the terms of this Act, occupational diseases mean the diseases specified in the schedule to the Act, provided that they are caused by employment in an insured undertaking of the kind mentioned in the schedule (list of diseases) opposite the occupational disease in question. The schedule is as follows:

Serial Number	Occupational Disease	Undertakings Insured Against Accidents
1	Diseases caused by lead and its compounds.	For serial numbers 1-13
2	Diseases caused by phosphorus and its compounds.	All undertakings in which the substances specified in the second column are manufactured, worked up or used or are found as by-products or in any other form.
3	Diseases caused by mercury and its compounds.	
4	Diseases caused by arsenic and its compounds	
5	Diseases caused by manganese and its compounds.	
6	Diseases caused by benzene and its homologues or by nitro and amido derivatives of the aromatic series.	
7	Diseases caused by carbon bisulphide.	
8	Diseases caused by sulphuretted hydrogen.	
9	Diseases by gases used in war, i. e. phosgene, thio, etc.	

Serial Number	Occupational Disease	Undertakings Insured Against Accidents
10	Diseases caused by carbon monoxide.	
11	Diseases caused by hydrocyanic acid or its derivatives, such as calcium cyanamide.	
12	Diseases caused by prolonged exposure to X-rays or to rays or other emanations of radium.	
13	Serious forms of eczema which are difficult to cure (cancer), caused by soot, paraffin, tar, creosote, anthracene, pitch and similar substances, and also the sequelae of such forms of eczema (cancer).	
14	Cancer of the lungs caused by radium rays and emanations.	Uranium mines and factories for the manufacture of uranium pigments, radium and radium preparations.
15	Anthrax	(a) Undertakings in which animals are kept or slaughtered or in which carcasses or waste products of animals liable to contract anthrax are used or destroyed. (b) Undertakings in which wool, hair skins, hides, horse-hair or bristles are worked up or in which trade in these materials is carried on or by which they are transported.
16	Infectious diseases	Institutions for the care of the sick.
17	Glanders	Undertakings in which insured persons are exposed to risk of this disease.
18	Diseases of the muscles, bones and joints of employees who use pneumatic drills, hammers, rivetting tools and other similar appliances	Undertakings in which such pneumatic machinery or apparatus is used.
19	Ankylostomiasis (miners' hookworm disease)	Mining undertakings.
20	Diseases of the respiratory system caused by the injurious effects of basic slag.	Undertakings in which basic slag is worked up or transported.

Serial Number	Occupational Disease	Undertakings Insured Against Accidents
21	Serious pneumoconiosis caused by quartz or iron dust. If serious pneumoconiosis occurs simultaneously with pulmonary tuberculosis, the tuberculosis shall for the purposes of compensation be deemed to be a disease caused by dust.	(a) Undertakings for quarrying, rough-working and finishing sandstone; (b) chinaware undertakings (c) undertakings for metal grinding; (d) mining undertakings in which the work is usually in hard quartz.
22	Diseases caused by chromium compounds.	Undertakings in which these compounds are used.
23	Deafness or hardness of hearing approximating to deafness, caused by noise and vibrations.	Undertakings for metal working or finishing.
24	Serious cataract	Glass works, iron works and foundries.
25	Serious and complicated forms of nystagmus.	Mining undertakings.

The beginning of the sickness within the meaning of the Acts respecting sickness insurance or the beginning of the incapacity for work within the meaning of the Acts respecting accident insurance, if this is more favorable to the insured person, or if the person concerned is not insured against sickness, is deemed to be equivalent to the date of the accident. In the case of an occupational disease, the compensation payable to a person insured against sickness consists of the pension due to the person suffering from the occupational disease, from the twenty-seventh week after the beginning of the sickness, or after the beginning of the incapacity for work, as the case may be.

The obligation to give notice of occupational disease within the statutory time limit is incumbent upon every sickness insurance carrier which becomes aware of the presence of any such disease. It may be prescribed by government order that the obligation to give notice of occupational diseases is also incumbent upon every medical practitioner who has diagnosed any such disease.

If there is any reason to fear that an occupational disease will recur or be aggravated if the insured person continues to be employed in an undertaking of the kind in question, the accident insurance carrier may grant him an appropriate temporary pension amounting to not more than half the full pension, if he gives up his employment in such undertaking. Receipt of this pension does not affect the claim to a pension on account of incapacity for work.

If a victim has not been automatically granted compensation, he must lodge his claim within a year of the date on which the presence of an occupational disease has been diagnosed by a medical practitioner, and not in any case more than two years after the date on which his employment in the undertaking specified ceased.

The surviving dependents of a person who has died in consequence of an occupational disease must lodge their claim within a year of the date of his death. The surviving dependents of a person whose claim has lapsed (because he failed to lodge his claim within a year of the date on which the presence of an occasional disease was diagnosed), are not entitled to compensation.

This Act is administered by the Minister of Social Welfare, and with respect to the Slovak Fund for Agricultural Workers at Bratislava, by the Minister of Agriculture, in agreement with the other Ministers concerned.

On September 19, 1932, Czechoslovakia ratified the Convention concerning workmen's compensation for occupational diseases,[11] adopted by the International Labor Conference at its seventh session in Geneva, 1925. Article I of the Convention provides that compensation shall be payable to workmen who are incapacitated by occupational diseases, or, in case of death from such diseases, to their dependents, in accordance with the general principles of the national legislation relating to compensation for industrial accidents. The rates of such compensation shall not be less than those prescribed by the national legislation for injury resulting from industrial accidents.

Article II provides that "Each Member of the International Labor Organization which ratifies this Convention undertakes to consider as occupational diseases those diseases and poisonings produced by the substances set forth in the Schedule appended hereto, when such diseases or such poisonings affect workers engaged in the trades or industries placed opposite in the said Schedule, and result from occupation in an undertaking covered by the said national legislation.

SCHEDULE

List of Diseases and Toxic Substances	List of Corresponding Industries and Processes
Poisoning by lead, its compounds or alloys, and their sequelae.	Handling of ore containing lead, including fine shot in zinc factories. Casting of old zinc and lead in ingots. Manufacture of articles made of cast lead or of lead alloys. Employment in the polygraphic industries. Manufacture of lead compounds. Manufacture and repair of electric accumulators. Preparation and use of enamels containing lead. Polishing by means of lead files or putty powder with a lead content. All painting operations involving the preparation and manipulation of coating substances, cements or coloring substances containing lead pigments.
Poisoning by mercury, its amalgams and compounds and their sequelae.	Handling of mercury ore. Manufacture of mercury compounds. Manufacture of measuring and laboratory apparatus. Preparation of raw material for the hat-making industry. Hot gilding. Use of mercury pumps in the manufacture of incandescent lamps. Manufacture of fulminate of mercury primers.

List of Diseases and Toxic Substances	List of Corresponding Industries and Processes
Anthrax infection.	Work in connection with animals infected with anthrax. Handling of animal carcasses or parts of such carcasses including hides, hoofs and horns. Loading and unloading or transport of merchandise.

On February 8, 1927, Czechoslovakia ratified the Convention concerning equality of treatment for national and foreign workers as regards workmen's compensation for accidents, which was also adopted at the seventh session of the International Labor Conference in Geneva in 1925. Article I of this Convention [12] states that, when a person to whom compensation is due under the laws and regulations of one Member resides in the territory of another Member, the necessary measures be taken to facilitate the payment of such compensation and to ensure the observance of the conditions governing such payment laid down by the said laws and regulations. This provision is carried out by the terms of the legislation of Czechoslovakia.[13]

The Convention concerning workmen's compensation for accidents, which was also adopted by the International Labor Conference at its seventh session in Geneva in 1925, has not been ratified by Czechoslovakia. Article II of the Convention [14] states that the laws and regulations as to workmen's compensation shall apply to workmen, employees and apprentices employed by any enterprise, undertaking or establishment of whatsoever nature, whether public or private. Exceptions may be made, however, in the case of:

(a) persons whose employment is of a casual nature;

(b) out-workers;

(c) members of the employer's family who work exclusively on his behalf and who live in his house;

(d) non-manual workers whose remuneration exceeds a limit to be determined by national laws or regulations.

This is more inclusive than the terms of the legislation of Czechoslovakia, which applies to a list of ten industrial and transportation undertakings, and which excludes from the scope of compulsory accident insurance: [15]

(a) undertakings temporarily employing machinery not forming part of their plant;

(b) the construction of dwelling houses and agricultural buildings in rural areas, provided that only the builder, the members of his family, and other persons living in the same commune, who are themselves not builders by trade, are employed on such work.

(2) LEGISLATION REGARDING THE USE OF WHITE LEAD, PHOSPHORUS, AND OTHER POISONOUS SUBSTANCES

A. In Austria Prior to 1918

The use of white lead in painting was regulated in Austria by the Order of April 15, 1908.[16] By this Order, regulations were made for the protection of persons employed in painting, varnishing, and decorating, carried on by way of trade. It provided that in all rooms of industrial establishments where painting, varnishing, or decorating processes were carried on, the floors and walls should be covered with a washable surface without cracks. In order to keep these workrooms in a state of cleanliness, the walls and floors were to be washed every day after working hours.

It was the duty of owners of industrial undertakings who employed more than twenty workmen in painting, varnishing, and in decorating, to provide suitable heated lavatories and cloakrooms containing accommodations for keeping the clothing of the workmen. Certain special working regulations were made. Paints, colors, and cement containing lead should be kept and used in vessels and cases on which the nature of their contents was clearly indicated.

No white lead or paints, colors, or cement containing lead might be used by way of trade for interior work. Women and young persons might not be employed in any work in which the use of white lead or lead compounds was allowed. Workmen whom the employer knew to be suffering from lead poisoning might not be employed again in processes in which white lead or lead compounds were used until they had been certified by a medical practitioner as being cured and fit for industrial employment. The crushing or grinding of lead or lead compounds and the kneading of such substances with oil or varnish should be done by mechanical apparatus and not by hand and under such conditions that the workmen would be adequately protected against the generation of dust.

The law provided that the employer should see that workmen who worked with lead or lead compounds wore special clothing and head coverings during work. In industrial undertakings where more than twenty persons were employed, the employer should provide the necessary clothing and head coverings and should have them cleaned periodically. No white lead or lead compounds should be kept or manipulated in the living rooms or bedrooms provided for the workmen.

By the Act of April 26, 1909,[17] the importation and sale of lead colors and cement was prohibited, unless the fact that they contained lead was expressly marked upon them in a clear and comprehensible manner. This Act was supplemented by the Circular of the Ministry of the Interior, dated December 17, 1913.

On July 13, 1909, an Act was passed relating to the manufacture of matches, in which the use of white or yellow phosphorus was prohibited. It stated that matches containing white or yellow phosphorus should not be offered for sale, sold, or circulated in any way. The Minister of Commerce, in agreement with the Minister of the Interior, was empowered to prohibit, for reasons of health or safety, or to allow, subject to certain conditions, the use of certain igniting pastes and striking surfaces in the manufacture of matches. The Minister of Commerce, in agreement with the Minister of the Interior, was also empowered to acquire possession of new processes for the manufacture of matches affording especially good guarantees for health and safety of workmen employed in the manufacture of matches and of the public, and to place such processes at the disposal of the manufacturers. The industrial inspectors might take from any establishment where matches of any kind were manufactured samples of the chemicals and pastes used in making matches or surfaces for striking matches, as well as of the finished goods.[18]

An Order was issued on May 24, 1909, respecting the obligation to obtain licenses for the manufacture of matches. It stated that matches should not be manufactured by way of trade except in pursuance of a license. The provincial authorities should grant such licenses after consultation with the Chambers of Commerce and Industry, provided that the conditions prescribed for the setting up of licensed business in general were present.[19]

B. In Hungary Prior to 1918

There were General Orders dated 1884 and 1893 regulating lead foundries, and General Orders and legislation dealing with the use of white and yellow phosphorus, and other poisonous substances, prior to 1918.[20] The Act of January 16, 1911,[21] prohibited the manufacture of matches from white or yellow phosphorus. It also prohibited the importation, storing, sale, or otherwise bringing on the market, of matches made from white or yellow phosphorus. The Minister of Commerce was authorized to prohibit, also, the use of other igniting agents or coatings which were dangerous to the health and safety of the workers.

The observance of the prohibition to use white or yellow phosphorus, as well as other materials prohibited in the manufacture of matches, was supervised by the industrial inspectors. These industrial inspectors were empowered to take samples of the materials used in the manufacture of matches, or of the finished products, from the match factories and warehouses which were under their supervision.

The duties of the industrial inspectors were stated in detail in the Order of December 31, 1912.[22] It provided that the inspectors were bound to inspect all match factories in order to ascertain whether the Act was being observed. Should they come to the conclusion that white or yellow phosphorus was being used in the manufacture of matches in a certain factory, they were bound to take a sample of suitable size of the matches in question. Should it be established that white or yellow phosphorus was being used, the Industrial Inspection service was bound to give immediate notice of penal proceedings against the person concerned.

An Order was issued on December 28, 1916,[23] respecting the protection and maintenance of health of workers employed in match factories. It provided that substances such as red phosphorus, chlorate of potash, sulphuretted antimony, etc., used in match factories for making the igniting mixture, should be kept in tightly covered, fireproof stores, entirely separate from the workrooms. Every room in which the producer stored chlorate of potash must be provided with a door leading into the open air, and be separated from places used for keeping the other substances. Chlorate of potash should be taken from the storerooms into the workrooms only in a closed vessel, immediately before the beginning of the process, and in such a quantity that it would be used on the same day.

The preparation of the igniting mixture (paste) and the removal of the substances necessary for this purpose from the storerooms should be entrusted only to reliable workers who knew the precautionary measures to be observed. Chlorate of potash and all the substances used in the manufacture of matches should be kept and used in such a manner that their dust could not penetrate into the air of the workrooms.

All workrooms must have sufficient fireproof entrances and exits of adequate size and suitably lit. All workrooms must be so arranged that they could be thoroughly aired as required.

A special lavatory must be provided in the immediate neighborhood of the workrooms. Washing appliances must be provided in such numbers, or so arranged, that at least one-fifth of the workers could wash at the same time. The employer should see that the workers employed in the processes wash their hands carefully and removed the clothes worn during work before taking food and before leaving the factory.

The employer should provide a special eating room for his workers and should see that the workers kept in it any food they might bring with them.

Workers under sixteen years of age might not be employed in preparing paste, or in putting the matches into the drying chambers or removing them therefrom.

C. In Czechoslovakia

In order to extend the provisions of the Austrian Order of April 15, 1908, to the remainder of the territory of Czechoslovakia, and to bring them into conformity with the International Labor Convention concerning the use of white lead in painting, the Act of June 12, 1924,[24] was passed, issuing regulations for the protection of the life and health of persons employed in painting, varnishing, and decorating. This act prohibits the use of white lead and other pigments and putty containing lead in internal painting, varnishing, and decorating work. Internal painting is defined as "all painting which, on account of the use to which it is put, is not exposed directly to the influence of the weather either permanently or during the greater part of the time." This prohibition, however, does not apply to (a) decoration, sign painting, and fine lining; (b) railway stations, vehicle works, and other industrial undertakings where the use of white lead is certified as necessary by the competent industrial inspection office after consultation with the organizations of workers and employers; (c) painting in places where the paint is exposed to the effects of steam or other vapors; and (d) work in the application of the first coat in cases of mere touching up of old white paint containing lead.

The exceptions under (c) and (d) were reproduced from the Order of April 15, 1908, after consultation with the organizations concerned, because of the similarity between interior painting exposed to steam and other vapors and external painting, and also because of the practical value of the second exception. As a result of research, zinc paints are almost exclusively used in interior painting, as they are non-poisonous, lasting, and permanently white. In the application of the first coat upon wood and for putty, zinc white is used mixed with a white lead substitute which is commercially known as "Lithopone". Permits to use white lead are granted by the Industrial Inspectorate, which gives notice of the permits granted to the competent industrial authority, this body being entitled to reverse the decision of the inspectorate. It also refers to this authority applications which it considers should be refused.

The employment of young persons under eighteen years of age and of women is prohibited in work where the use of white lead and other pigments and putty containing lead is permitted. The competent industrial inspection offices are empowered, after consulting the organizations of employers and workers, to "permit the employment of apprentices under eighteen years of age on work otherwise prohibited for them by the provisions of this act, with a view to their training in their trade, in so far as this work is necessary for the full achievement of the purpose of their apprenticeship, provided that they shall not be so employed for more than six weeks." The competent authority must be notified if such permits are granted, and this authority is entitled to reverse the decision of the inspectorate.

The employer must provide the workers with suitable respirators for work involving the raising of dust. Dry paint or putty containing lead must not be scraped or rubbed down until it has been dampened. The scraped-off substance and the fragments falling during the process of scraping must be removed while still damp. In industrial undertakings employing not less than fifteen workers a separate lavatory, capable of being heated, must be supplied. Workers using white lead or other pigments, putty, and similar substances containing lead must be provided by the employer with suitable wash bowls. Hot water is made available wherever possible, also soap, nail brushes, and a towel for each worker. The workers must wash their faces, mouths, and hands thoroughly before meals and when work is over.

The employer must see that the workers wear special working clothes and head coverings, and in undertakings usually employing not less than fifteen workers, he must provide the working clothes and also provide for their cleaning at his expense. In undertakings usually employing not less than fifteen workers, a separate cloakroom capable of being heated must be provided, with suitable arrangements made for storing working clothes and outdoor clothes separately. In establishments with a smaller number of workers, the workers are provided with clothes-lockers which can be securely closed and which are arranged so that working clothes and outdoor clothes can be kept apart.

A worker who shows signs of lead poisoning must be sent at once by the employer to the sick fund medical officer. If a worker is certified as suffering from lead poisoning, the employer must submit to the competent authority without delay a copy of the relevant particulars contained in the register which is kept of workers using white lead. The district or communal medical officer must examine any worker known or suspected to be suffering from lead poisoning and report his observations to the industrial authority. The employer is required to see that the workers usually engaged in handling white lead are given a medical examination at least once in six months. The result of each examination must be entered in the register kept by the employer.

Official statistical records are kept of the cases of lead poisoning observed and of the amount of sickness and mortality among workers employed in handling lead or substances containing lead. A special Committee for the technical and hygienic protection of workers has been created in the Ministry of Social Welfare as a consultative body attached to it. The factory inspectors and the district and communal medical officers are entrusted with the supervision of the act.

On August 31, 1923, Czechoslovakia ratified the Convention concerning the use of white lead in painting,[25] which was adopted by the International Labor Conference at its third session in Geneva in 1921. In all except two minor instances, the Act of June 12, 1924, regulating the use of white lead in painting, complies exactly with the provisions of the Convention.

Subsections (c) and (d) under Article 2 of the Czechoslovak law state that the prohibition of white lead and other pigments and putty containing lead shall not apply to painting in places where the paint is much exposed to the effects of steam or other vapors, and in work in the application of the first coat in cases of mere touching up of old white paint containing lead. The Ministry of Social Welfare in Czechoslovakia considers that, although these exceptions are not in accordance with the White Lead Convention, their application in practice is so unimportant that it constitutes only an insignificant and theoretical departure from the Convention. In practice, paints containing lead are used in interior painting to the extent allowed by the Geneva Convention (2 per cent) only occasionally, in putty, when it is desired to obtain a specially hard and damp-resisting surface. Suppression of the exceptions is not considered desirable, since their inclusion has met the requirements of the Committee of Experts at the International Labor Office.

---

1 *Twenty-fourth Annual Report of the Commissioner of Labor, 1909* (Washington: Government Printing Office, 1911), I, 36.

2 Information regarding Workmen's Compensation in Hungary taken from *Compensation for Industrial Accidents*, Studies & Reports, Series M, No. 2 (I. L. O., Geneva, Switzerland, 1925), p. 49; also, *Workmen's Compensation*

Legislation of the U. S. & Foreign Countries (U. S. Dept. of Labor Statistics Bulletin No. 126 [1914]), p. 151.

3 *International Survey of Social Services. 1933* (I. L. O., Geneva, Switz., 1936), p. 119.

4 *Op. cit.*, p. 121.

5 *Official Bulletin*, VIII, 11; also, *International Survey of Social Service, 1933*, p. 123.

6 *Industrial and Labor Information*, XLVI, 328.

7 *Industrial and Labor Information*, XLIII, 43.

8 *Industrial and Labor Information*, XLIX, 52.

9 *Ibid.*, LXI, 340.

10 *Legislative Series*, 1932, Cz. 1.

11 *Official Bulletin*, X, 110.

12 For the text of the Convention concerning equality of treatment, see *Official Bulletin*, X, 117.

13 See *supra*, p. 104.

14 For the text of the Convention concerning workmen's compensation for accidents, see *Official Bulletin*, X, 103.

15 See *supra*, pp. 97, 98.

16 *Bulletin of the International Labor Office*, Basle, Switzerland: III [1908], 31. Note the following measures relative to lead in Austria before 1908: G. O., March 8, 1885, § 74a, requiring employers to adopt measures to safeguard the life and health of workers—workrooms, machinery, tools, license for factory premises (special patent); Measures of protection for working painters: Kundmachung des Verwaltung der I. des Werfte. Donau Dampfschiffahrts-Gesellschaft in Korneburg, 1886. (Proclamation of the Docks Management Board of the 1 Danube Steamship Company at Korneburg, 1886,; Order of the Governor of Lower Austria relative to colors containing white lead. Application to buildings August 27, 1906; Resolution of the Municipal Council (Vienna) relative to the prohibition of white lead colors and red lead in municipal works, March 5, 1907.—Information received from the I. L. O., Geneva, Switzerland.

17 *Bulletin of the International Labor Office*, Basle, Switzerland, IV [1909], 71.

18 *Op. cit.*, IV [1909], 186. Note the following Measures relative to phosphorus in Austria before 1909: Ministerial Decree of the State Council of September 3, 1846 (in Lower Austria and Bohemia); G. O. dated December 20, 1859 to March 15, 1883, § 27, containing prohibition to set up match factories unless a license to do so had been previously obtained from the Factory Administration (special patent); Ministerial Order dated January 17, 1885, of the Ministry of the Interior and the Ministry of Commerce in regard to the measures to be taken relative to the protection of the workers'

health in workrooms intended for the manufacture of chemical matches. Such measures to be taken on the basis of proposals made by the Superior Health Council.—Information received from the I. L. O., Geneva, Switzerland.

19 *Op. cit.*, IV [1909], 185.

20 Illustrative of such Orders and legislation up to 1911, are the following: Circular Order of the Ministry of the Interior, No. 24929, dated March 27, 1898 relative to the protection of the health of workers in match factories, which was based on §§ 6, 15, 156 (G. O. XIV, 1876), 1 (G. O. XXVIII, 1893), 116 (G. O. XVII, 1884) and repealed the Order relative to the protection of the health of workers in match factories, No. 5089, dated March 15, 1869; Appendix No. 24929, 1908 containing regulations relative to the protection of the health of workers in match factories; Order of the Ministry of the Interior No. 101868, dated Dec. 2, 1899 (relative to insufficient prophylaxis in match factories); and Appendix No. 101868/1898 containing supplementary provisions to the Order of the Ministry of the Interior, No. 78904/1898, dated April 18, 1899.—Information received from the I. L. O., Geneva, Switzerland.

21 *Op. cit.*, VII [1912], 209.

22 *Op. cit.*, X, 12.

23 *Ibid.*, XII, 62.

24 *Legislative Series*, 1924, Cz. 1.

25 For the text of the Convention concerning the use of white lead in painting, see *Official Bulletin*, IV, 13.

CHAPTER VII

UNEMPLOYMENT INSURANCE

A. In Austria Prior to 1918

The unemployment insurance legislation of Austria prior to 1918 was an adaptation of the so-called Ghent system. Starting in Ghent in 1900 under the direction of Mr. Louis Varlez, this was the first successful method of organizing social unemployment insurance.

The principle underlying the Ghent system was public subsidy to labor organizations granting out-of-work benefits. The purpose was to increase the amount of the benefits given, without additional cost to the wage-earner, and to stimulate other unions to organize such systems. With this purpose in view, a certain appropriation was made by the municipality of Ghent, together with its suburbs. From that appropriation, subsidies were granted to all organizations giving employment benefits. The amount of the subsidy was in proportion to the labor union benefits, and was determined periodically, according to the funds available and the general level of unemployment. This proportion was usually 60 per cent of the original benefit.

There were several limitations. The amount of the subsidy could not exceed 100 per cent of the original benefit. The subsidy was computed only on the first daily franc of the benefit. It was not given for more than sixty days in any one year to one unemployed person. Subsidy was paid only in respect of involuntary unemployment, including unemployment due to a breakdown of machinery or to a fire at a factory. It was not granted when the unemployment was due to a strike or lockout, or to sickness or other physical incapacity. It was paid only to persons residing in the communes participating in the scheme.

The Ghent system with various modifications was later adopted by many communities throughout Europe. Not only municipalities, but states, made appropriations for subsidizing trade union unemployment funds.[1] The system in operation in Austria closely resembled this Ghent system. In 1909, over £71,000 was paid out by the social democratic trade unions in unemployment benefit, including traveling benefit. Some unemployment benefit was also paid by the "Christian Trade Unions."[2]

Austria was also active in the establishment of public and other employment bureaus in many of its provinces. The results were difficult to analyze and tabulate, because of the unusual variety of methods adopted for their organization in different portions of the Empire. There were six principal classes of employment bureaus, and many variations in each class.

A great deal of work was also done in securing positions by the relief shelters (Verpflegungsstationen), which were copied from Germany. They were started in Austria as early as 1887, and were organized into a general system of homes or hotels for workmen, especially those who were traveling in search of work. At these shelters, workers could find lodging for a night or two, either by paying a small sum or, if unable to pay, by doing a little work in the morning. They were, in all cases, private institutions, maintained by the trade unions, or not infrequently, by religious societies.

In 1903, there were five public employment bureaus, of which the Vienna bureau was by far the most important. It had several branches, and was very active in finding work, especially in factories and industries in which no guild existed. Every week, a list of the applications for employment and for help was classified according to trades and printed and posted in all the districts of the city. Applicants were sent to employers, as a rule, in the order of their application, but precedence was given to those having a legal residence in Vienna, as well as to those having children dependent upon them, or having other special needs.

This bureau proved so satisfactory that, at the end of the first year, forty of the trade guilds handed over their employment agencies to it, and by 1902 this number had increased to forty-six. In 1903, the work of the bureau was extended to domestic service, and in the same year eleven district employment offices were opened for women servants and one for men servants. Some of the trade unions exacted a fee from their members to cover expenses, but otherwise the bureau was free, no payment being asked from either employees or employers, except that employers in the domestic branch were charged a small registration fee.

The Prague municipal employment bureau was next to that of Vienna in importance and was conducted on practically the same plan. The bureau was managed by a committee composed of a chairman, who was a member of and appointed by the town council, three members of the executive committee of the town council, three representatives of the employers appointed by the town council, three representatives of the employed, actually employed in Prague, an inspector of relief stations appointed by the Bohemian provincial council, and the director in chief of the poor law administration. All the Bohemian bureaus were particularly noteworthy for being organized systematically.

In the province of Bohemia, the whole matter of unemployment exchanges was regulated by a Social Welfare Act of March 29, 1903, by which the country was divided into five regions with five regional employment exchanges working through 238 offices created by the districts and municipalities. The central labor office at Prague and the five regional offices were subsidized by the province of Bohemia, the other offices by the districts and municipalities.

In Moravia, there was no legal basis for employment exchanges. There were, however, twenty-eight offices created and maintained by the towns in which they were situated. The district of Brno labor office took the initiative in standardizing the whole employment exchange policy of the province by the issue of advice and general principles.

In Silesia, a central labor office was set up by a Ministerial Order of December 24, 1917. Aside from this central labor office, there were, in Silesia, 15 employment exchanges of which three only were maintained by the State and the province, the others being financed by the municipalities which set them up. There was also in Silesia an agricultural employment office situated at Opava, the expenses of which were borne by the Ministry of Agriculture and by the local agricultural employers' organization.[3]

B. In Hungary Prior to 1918

The same system of subsidizing trade union unemployment benefits was used in Hungary. On January 1, 1909, there were 49 social democratic trade unions with 102,000 members, and these unions paid, in 1908, 19,000 crowns in unemployment benefit of various kinds. In addition, a national union of commercial employees established an unemployment benefit fund in July 1909.[4]

In order to bring the demand for and the supply of labor into adjustment in all branches of industrial work, as well as in mining and commerce, Act No. XVI of 1916[5] provided that towns and communes designated for this purpose should be bound to provide official employment bureaus. Some towns were required to provide employment bureaus with a sphere of operations extending beyond their own territory. These might be granted an annual subvention by the Minister of Commerce. In determining this subvention, the valuation of property, the size of the territory over which it had jurisdiction for the purpose of the employment bureau, and the number of persons resident within this territory who were employed in industry, mining and commerce, were to be the determining factors.

The official employment bureaus were to be entirely free, both to employers and to workers. The Minister of Commerce, in agreement with the Minister of the Interior, determined the towns and communes where it was compulsory for official employment bureaus to be provided, to define their sphere of operations, and to regulate their organization and management.

C. In Czechoslovakia

Unemployment insurance in Czechoslovakia is governed by the Act of July 19, 1921,[6] as amended and supplemented by the Act of June 5, 1930,[7] respecting the State supplement to unemployment benefit.

1. SCOPE

Under the terms of these acts, nationals of the Czechoslovak Republic who are liable to compulsory sickness insurance may acquire the right to a State supplement to benefit during unemployment. Also, nationals of a foreign State may receive the State supplement under the same conditions as nationals of the Czechoslovak Republic, provided that the foreign State has analogous institutions and treats Czechoslovak nationals in the same way as its own nationals. Also, members of trade organizations which grant benefit to its members during unemployment are entitled to the State supplement.

Not included are:

(a) persons who are not entitled to unemployment benefit under the rules of the trade organization;

(b) persons who are entitled to unemployment benefit under the rules of the trade organization, but who have not been members thereof for three months before the date of their becoming unemployed;

(c) persons who are on strike or locked out;

(d) persons who have been dismissed from employment, or who have voluntarily left their employment without sufficient reason;

(e) persons who are incapable of regular work on account of their physical or mental condition;

(f) persons who are in receipt of sick benefits from a sick fund;

(g) persons living outside the territory of Czechoslovakia;

(h) seasonal workers. The Government may, by Order, extend the operation of this Act to particular groups of seasonal workers, and lay down special conditions for them in respect to the basis, duration, and amount of the State supplement.

The right to the State supplement during unemployment is forfeited by any person:

(a) who has forfeited the right to unemployment benefit under the rules of the trade organization;

(b) who has refused employment offered to him by a public or trade employment exchange, although he is capable of performing the offered work, which is not of such a kind as to endanger his qualification for his own occupation, and is paid for according to the wage scale in force or at the rate customary in the locality where the work is to be performed;

(c) who has refused to perform temporary work of public utility, assigned to him by an employment exchange, for a period corresponding to that for which a sum equal to the State supplement for unemployment benefit due to him would constitute the weekly wages, although he is capable of performing the work;

(d) who has received the State supplement during unemployment for twenty-six weeks in one year, if the trade organization pays benefits during unemployment in weekly installments, or for six months if the organization pays benefits in monthly installments. These periods of twenty-six weeks and six months respectively, are reckoned from the first day of unemployment.

2. ADMINISTRATION

A committee of the trade organization decides as to the granting, refusal, or suspension of unemployment benefit and the State supplement. The trade organization is bound to submit its transactions in connection with the State supplement to State supervision which is exercised by the Minister of Social Welfare and the Minister of Finance.

3. BENEFITS

The State supplement is equal to three times the benefit paid by the trade organization, out of its own funds, to the claimant. In the case of married members who have been members of the trade organization for not less than one year, and in the case of unmarried members who have been members of the organization for five years, the State supplement amounts to four times the benefit paid by the organization. The Minister of Social Welfare has power to grant this supplement, equal to four times the benefit paid by the organization, to unmarried members in deserving cases, if the members maintain their children and do not draw any regular allowance in respect of them, or if they are maintaining parents who are more than 65 years of age.

The State supplement to the benefit paid by the trade organization must not exceed 18 crowns a day, and the total amount of the benefit and the State supplement must not exceed two-thirds of the last wages received by the unemployed person. An unemployed person is entitled to the State supplement during twenty-six weeks of unemployment in one year, from the day on which he applies for it, provided that he has been unemployed for not less than seven consecutive days.

A member of a trade organization who has exhausted his claim to benefit during unemployment, and to the State supplement, has a claim for a further period of not more than thirteen weeks in the same benefit year, provided that the benefit paid by the organization is not less than .40 crowns a day. In this case, the State supplement amounts to 1.60 crowns a day. If the benefit paid by the organization exceeds .40 crowns, the State supplement amounts to three times or four times the benefit paid by the organization, as the case may be, provided that the total amount of this benefit and the State supplement is not less than 2 crowns. The State supplement is increased by the amount by which the total is less than the aforesaid amounts.

A member of a trade organization who has not yet acquired a claim to benefit during unemployment in conformity with the rules of the trade organization, or who has already exhausted his claim to benefit and to the State supplement, is entitled to extraordinary benefit during unemployment and to a State supplement for thirteen weeks in the year, if, as a result of prolonged unfavorable conditions in the labor market, he is unemployed without any fault of his own and if his own livelihood and that of his family are endangered thereby.

The benefit paid by a trade organization from its funds, in case of exceptional unemployment, must not be less than .25 crowns a day, and the State supplement to the benefit paid by the organization, in such case, must not be less than 1.75 crowns a day. If the benefit paid by the organization exceeds .25 crowns, the State supplement is increased by three or four times the increase in the benefit paid by the organization. In order to establish his claim to this benefit, the unemployed person is bound to register for employment at the competent public employment exchange. If the employment exchange cannot procure suitable employment for the unemployed person, it must issue to him a certificate to that effect.

From the funds allocated for combating unemployment, the Minister of Social Welfare may make grants to emergency relief works undertaken in the public interest by the State, a province, a district, a commune, or a public corporation. Persons who are in receipt of benefit and the State supplement during unemployment, are given preference in employment on such work. The State makes a grant amounting to not more than 10 crowns a day toward the payment of wages of persons taken from the ranks of the unemployed and assigned to emergency relief works.

Czechoslovakia has not ratified the Convention concerning unemployment adopted by the International Labor Conference at its first session in Washington in 1919. Article II of this Convention [8] provides that "each Member which ratifies this Convention shall establish a system of free public employment agencies under the control of a central authority. Committees, which shall include representatives of employers and of workers, shall be appointed to advise on matters concerning the carrying on of these agencies. Where both public and private free employment agencies exist, steps shall be taken to coordinate the operations of such agencies on a national scale."

This has not been provided for in the legislation of Czechoslovakia. In regard to employment exchanges, there has been in Slovakia, since 1919, a labor office for agricultural workers, situated at Bratislava, and eight department exchanges maintained by the Ministry of Agriculture. The placing of other categories of workers in that province is carried out by means of provincial offices, and eight exchanges financed by the towns and by the State. The employment exchanges of the other provinces, Bohemia, Moravia, and Silesia, continued under Czechoslovak rule the work they were doing under the Austro-Hungarian Empire. In 1931, the Minister of Social Welfare drafted a bill providing for a Central Labor Office, assisted by a joint advisory committee of twelve members and a central vocational guidance office. This bill was laid before the National Assembly, but the records do not show that any action has been taken upon it to date.

---

1 I. M. Rubinow, "Subsidized Unemployment Insurance," *Journal of Political Economy* (Chicago: University of Chicago Press, 1913), XXI, 412-431.

2 I. G. Gibbon, *Unemployment Insurance* (London: P. S. King & Son, Orchard House, Westminster, 1911), p. 29.

3 W. D. F. Bliss, *What is Done for the Unemployed in European Countries* (Bureau of Labor Statistics, Bulletin No. 76 [1908], pp. 741-934; *Industrial and Labor Information*, XX, 174.

4 I. G. Gibbon, *Unemployment Insurance* (London: P. S. King and Son, 1911), p. 29.

5 Bulletin of *International Labor Office*, Basle, XI [1916], 22.

6 *Legislative Series*, 1921, Cz. 5.

7 *Ibid.*, 1930, Cz. 1.

8 For the text of the Convention concerning unemployment see *Official Bulletin*, I, 417.

PART III

OTHER ASPECTS OF LABOR LEGISLATION; SUMMARY AND CONCLUSION

CHAPTER VIII

(1) PARTICIPATION OF WORKERS IN MANAGEMENT

By the Act of February 25, 1920,[1] a works council was instituted for each independent undertaking in the mining industry in which not less than twenty workers were employed, and which had existed for not less than six months. The duties of the councils are to cooperate with the inspection authorities in the execution and observance of agreements regarding wages and salaries. The councils assist in maintaining discipline, take action in case of complaints, intervene in the dismissal of workers, administer welfare schemes for workers, and examine the annual balance sheet of the undertaking.

The members of the works councils are elected by direct and secret vote of all persons employed in the works, irrespective of sex, provided they have been employed for not less than three months in the works and are at least eighteen years of age. Persons are eligible to the works council, who have been employed in the mining industry in the district concerned for not less than three years and have completed their twenty-fourth year of age.

The law also provides for a district council which is elected by the works councils of each separate mining district. The district council has ten members, if not more than 10,000 workers are employed in the district; fifteen members for not more than 15,000; twenty members for not more than 20,000; and so on up to thirty-five members for not more than 50,000 workers in the district. Eligibility for the district councils is subject to the same conditions as for the works council, provided that one-fifth of the members must be representative of the salaried employees, and one-fourth may, if desired, be representatives of trade organizations of wage-earning and salaried employees.

The duties of the district council are to establish principles for the whole district in respect to the carrying out of the duties of the works councils; to decide in case of dispute between a works management and a works council; to assist in the conclusion of collective agreements regarding wages and labor conditions after these have been discussed by the trade organizations, and to supervise their observance; to assist in conciliation; to assist in determining the price and distribution of coal; to decide as to the application of the share of the net profits allocated to the district council for use in the general interests of the workers; and to make reports concerning its activities and their financial results, not less than once a year.

All persons employed in the mining industry to whom this act applies are entitled to participate in the management of the undertaking and in the allocation of a share of the net profits. The share of the profits due to the employees is fixed at 10% of the net profits which are allocated for distribution among the shareholders. The share allocated to the employees is paid to the district council for the district in which the mines in question are situated, in the proportion which the net profits of these mines bear to the general profits of the district.

Joint management of mining undertakings is provided for in all undertakings which permanently employ more than one hundred persons. The employees participate in the management of the undertaking through their representatives on the joint council of the undertaking. This joint council fixes the amount of the employees' share in the net profits. The employer has to submit to the joint council a quarterly report on the past financial year, the balance sheet and profit and loss statement, and a proposal as to the division of the net profits.

The joint council consists of seven members, of whom two are chosen from the wage-earning, and one from the salaried employees. The employer nominates the remaining members. The representatives of the employees on the joint council are elected by all the works councils from among their own members by direct and secret vote. Only those persons are eligible for the joint council who have been employed in the same undertaking for not less than two years and in the mining industry in the district in question for not less than four years. They must be at least thirty years of age.

The Act of February 25, 1920, as amended by the Act of July 3, 1924,[2] set up Mining Arbitration Courts at the seats of the district councils. Each mining arbitration court consists of two representatives of the employers, two representatives of the salaried employees, two representatives of the wage-earning employees, and a chairman.

Mining arbitration courts have sole competence in the appeals of the works council or the works management against the decision of the district councils in disputes between works management and works council; appeals of the works council against dismissal of an employee without notice, if dismissal took place without the consent of the works council; appeals of employees against decisions of the works council in disputes respecting wages and salaries, and respecting the termination of employment; applications of works management to terminate employment of members of a works or district council. The mining arbitration court also has sole competence in matters relating to wages and salaries, complaints relating to discipline, and to the dismissal of employees from undertakings in which there is no works council. Appeals are decided by the Superior Arbitration Court, the decision of which is final. This Court consists of three professional judges, one of whom is chairman, and two assessors, one from each of the groups concerned.

In regard to other undertakings beside mining, the Act of August 12, 1921,[3] provided that a works committee be established for every independent undertaking carried on for profit, in which not less than thirty workers are employed regularly, and which has been in existence for not less than half a year.

It is the duty of works committees to watch over and promote the economic, social, and intellectual interests of the employees. In particular, they see that contracts and rules concerning wages and employment are observed, that arrangements agreed upon before conciliation boards and awards of arbitration boards are put into operation and observed, especially those dealing with accident prevention, hygienic measures, and the insurance of employees; and that discipline and order are maintained in the works.

The committee does not interfere in the management or operation of the undertaking by giving independent orders, but carries out all its assigned duties in such a way as not to hamper the operation of the works. In order to help the works committee fulfil its duties, the works management transmits to it copies of labor contracts and rules of employment, notifies it of the proceedings of committees and of the visits of inspection officials, and at least every three months presents to the works committee a report on the commercial and administrative situation of the works, its output, and its prospects. The works committee is entitled to send delegates to the meetings of the board of management, but only those members of the works committee can act as delegates who are at least thirty years of age and have been employed in the works for not less than three years. These delegates are not entitled to vote.

In an undertaking where there are at least thirty and not more than sixty employees, the works committee consists of three members; where there are from sixty-one to one hundred employees, it consists of four members. One member is added to the committee for every 100 additional employees up to 400, one for every additional 200 from 401 to 1000 employees, one for every additional 500 from 1001 to 4000, and one for every additional 2000 above 4000 employees. In any case, the works committee may not have more than twenty members.

Any national of the Czechoslovak Republic is eligible to the works committee provided that he has attained the age of twenty-six years and has been employed for not less than twelve months in the undertaking in question, and that he has worked in the particular branch of industry or occupation for not less than three years. The term of office is one year.

Complaints and disputes between groups of employees, and between employees and the employer respecting the establishment and activities of the works committee, the defrayal of its expenses, and the extent of the rights and duties of the members of the works committee, are decided finally by the arbitration board. This arbitration board consists of six members, including two representatives each of the employers and the employees, an expert on social or economic questions, and a professional judge experienced in industrial matters. The decisions of this arbitration board are enforceable by law.

The Act of July 4, 1931,[4] provided for the creation of labor courts. These labor courts are not competent to deal with disputes which are within the jurisdiction of the bodies set up by the Act of February 25, 1920, respecting works and district councils in the mining industry, nor do they have any connection with the mining arbitration courts established by the Act of July 3, 1924, nor with the works committees created by the Act of August 12, 1921.

Subject to these limitations, labor courts are competent to give judgment in disputes between an employee and an employer or between employees of the same employer arising out of an employment, service, or apprenticeship, based on a private contract, irrespective of the sum involved. Specifically, the labor courts give judgment in disputes respecting wages, commission, and other payments arising out of employment; respecting the beginning, continuance, and termination of an employment, service, or apprenticeship; respecting claims arising out of membership in social insurance institutions or benefit funds; respecting notice to leave, the vacating, or rent of dwellings the use of which has been granted by the employer to the employee either free of charge or for payment; and respecting claims brought against each other by employees of the same employer which arise out of their employment.

The labor court consists of a chairman, a vice-chairman, and the requisite number of assessors and substitutes. The chairman and vice-chairman are appointed by the Minister of Justice, from among the professional judges exercising their functions at the seat of the labor court. The number of assessors is fixed by the Minister of Justice, and they are appointed by the President of the Superior Court in the area in which the labor court is situated. Half the assessors represent the employers and half represent the employees. Any Czechoslovak national to whom the provisions of this Act apply and who is at least thirty years of age may be appointed assessor of a labor court.[5]

(2) EMIGRATION

An act respecting emigration was passed on February 15, 1922,[6] and came into force three months after the date of its promulgation, on March 13, 1922. This act defines an emigrant as a person leaving the territory of the Czechoslovak Republic in order to earn his living abroad or with the intention of not returning. Emigration is free except for certain restrictions as to age, military service obligations, etc. Part I of the act provides that the Minister of Social Welfare shall make suitable regulations for the supply of information, in order to prevent the misleading of people in respect of prospects for work in other countries.

Part II of the act deals with the question of recruiting of settlers and workers to go abroad. Settlers may not be recruited without special permission of the Ministry of Social Welfare. The recruiting of labor for European countries is only authorized by consent of the State Office of Labor, and only through the medium of the Office of Labor on the basis of a written labor agreement which must conform with certain regulations laid down in the act.

Part III contains provisions with regard to the transport of emigrants. Only persons authorized by the Ministry of Social

Welfare may engage in the transport of emigrants. The transport undertaking or "carrier" must submit to State supervision and inspection, and may transport emigrants only after a carrier's permit has been granted by the Minister of Social Welfare. The Act also provides that an inspector chosen by the Minister of Social Welfare must be carried twice a year on vessels transporting emigrants.

Other provisions for the protection of emigrants deal with conditions such as food, medical aid, insurance, etc.; the reimbursement of the passage money and repatriation of emigrants in the event of delay or of continuation of the journey being impossible; the repatriation of Czechoslovak subjects without means who have been sent home by a Czechoslovak authority for any reason; and the sale of tickets for further transportation from an overseas port.

By the final provisions of the act, the Government is empowered to conclude conventions with other States concerning the protection of emigrants. The Government is also authorized to promulgate decrees concerning the admission to and passage across Czechoslovakia of emigrants of other countries. The Ministry of Social Welfare is responsible for supervising the enforcement of the law.

Regulations for the enforcement of the Emigration Act of February 15, 1922, were promulgated on June 8, 1922.[7] They state that a permanent emigration council shall be appointed at the Ministry of Social Welfare, consisting of representatives of employers, workers, migration experts, transportation undertakings, humanitarian undertakings, the State Land Office, the Statistical Office, Shipping Companies, and of all the Government Departments. This Council, nominated for a period of three years, acts as an advisory body to the government in all questions concerning emigration, immigration, and re-emigration. It appoints a standing committee of five members, which prepare material for the sittings of the Council and deal with all urgent matters during the time when the Council is not sitting.

All transportation undertakings which desire to engage in subsidized emigration must obtain a special license from the Ministry of Social Welfare, and in their application must state who is to pay the cost of the transport and the name of the undertaking for which the emigrant is going to work.

Detailed rules are laid down with regard to the contract which the transportation undertaking must conclude with the emigrant. Close supervision must be exercised by the Czechoslovak authorities over the safety apparatus and sanitary conditions of all emigrant ships carrying Czechoslovak citizens. Every emigrant must be examined by an official doctor before he leaves the country, in order to ensure as far as possible, admission to the country of immigration.

Special restrictions may be imposed on the transit of emigrants through Czechoslovakia to other countries, if as a result some of them are liable to become a public charge, or if, for some other reason, special regulations are considered necessary. All transportation undertakings must periodically send to the State Statistical Office extracts from their books, publications, and announcements.

No change in this legislation was necessary to enable Czechoslovakia, on May 25, 1928, to ratify the Convention concerning the simplification of the inspection of emigrants on board ship,[8] which was adopted by the eighth session of the International Labor Conference at Geneva in 1926.

(3) HOLIDAYS WITH PAY

Holidays with pay for employed persons in general were introduced by the Act of April 3, 1925.[9] Prior to that date, special measures were passed for commercial employees, under the Act of January 16, 1910,[10] and for miners under the Act of April 1, 1921.[11] An act providing holidays with pay for salaried employees became law on July 11, 1934.[12]

A. Holidays with Pay for Employed Persons in General

Persons who perform work or service in virtue of a contract of employment of service, and not as a subsidiary or casual occupation, are entitled to holidays with pay at the employer's expense. The provisions of the act do not apply to seasonal workers, agricultural or forestry workers paid by the day, home workers, commercial workers, or miners.

An annual holiday of six days with pay is granted to workers after at least one year's uninterrupted employment in the same undertaking, or with the same employer, After ten years' uninterrupted employment, annual leave amounts to seven days a year, and after fifteen years, to eight days. Apprentices are entitled to eight days a year after six months in the same undertaking. The Sunday and holidays occurring during the leave period are included therein.

Military service and the time lost by an employed person on account of sickness, accident, or any other reason not caused intentionally, or through gross neglect, are included in the period of employment giving right to a holiday. During the holiday period, employed persons are entitled to a remuneration corresponding to their average earnings for the four weeks immediately preceding the beginning of the leave period. Output bonuses are not paid during annual leave.

B. Holidays with Pay for Commercial Employees

Persons employed in a commercial undertaking mainly on commercial work or on higher grade work, and persons employed mainly on such work in the establishments scheduled in the act, are entitled to holidays with pay at the employer's expense.

An annual holiday of at least ten consecutive days is granted to employees after at least six months' uninterrupted service in the same undertaking; after five years' employment the annual holiday amounts to two weeks, and after fifteen years, to at least three weeks. Time lost on account of sickness or accident is not deducted from the holiday period. Employees continue to receive their full wages during the holiday period.

C. Holidays with Pay for Miners

Persons employed in reserved mining undertakings, or in attached undertakings, are entitled to an annual holiday of five days after one year's uninterrupted employment in the same mining district; after five years' service in the same district, the holiday period amounts to seven days, after ten years to ten days, and after fifteen years to twelve days. The Sunday and holidays occurring during the leave period are included therein. Military service and the time lost on account of sickness are included in the period of employment giving right to a holiday.

During the holiday period, the worker receives remuneration corresponding to each day's wage, including all usual supplements with the exception of output bonuses. Workers paid at job rates receive remuneration equal to their average earnings, others receiving wages equal to those of the class to which they belong.

D. Holidays with Pay for Salaried Employees

After six months' service in the same undertaking, the employee is entitled to two weeks' leave. After five years' service, the annual holiday amounts to three weeks, and after fifteen years' service to four weeks. For this period of leave, the employee is entitled to his money salary and also to an allowance in lieu of any payment in kind which he is unable to receive.

---

1 *Legislative Series*, 1920, Cz. 3-5.

2 *Legislative Series*, 1924, Cz. 2.

3 *Legislative Series*, 1921, Cz. 4.

4 *Legislative Series*, 1931, Cz. 3.

5 For more details concerning the participation of workers in management, see the following I. L. O. publications: *International Labor Review*, II, 26; *Studies and Reports*, Series A, No. 34, 1933, p. 307.

6 *Legislative Series*, 1922, Cz. 1.

7 *Industrial and Labor Information*, III, 551.

8 For the text of the Convention concerning the simplification of the inspection of emigrants, see *Official Bulletin*, XI, 139.

9 *Legislative Series*, 1925, Cz. 2.

10 *Bulletin of International Labor Office*, Basle, V [1910], 202.

11 *Legislative Series*, 1921, Cz. 3.

12 *Industrial and Labor Information*, LI, 297.

CHAPTER IX

CZECHOSLOVAKIA AND THE INTERNATIONAL LABOR ORGANIZATION

FROM the beginning of its existence as an independent state Czechoslovakia showed an active interest in labor legislation and its adoption along international lines. Through its representative on the Commission on International Labor Legislation appointed by the Paris Peace Conference on January 31, 1919, which held its first meeting at the Ministry of Labor in Paris, in February 1919, Czechoslovakia submitted a "Memorial of the Czech Delegation About the Eight Hour Day".[1] In this document, it was stated that, in as much as Czechoslovakia had already on December 19, 1918, accepted the eight hour day law in all its factories, commercial, transportation, and agricultural concerns, it was interested in the internationalization and general acceptance of the eight-hour day. Arguments were given to prove that such action was necessary to bring about social justice and permanent peace throughout the countries of the world. Statistics of conditions in various countries were quoted to show that the adoption of the eight-hour day would result in greater rather than less productiveness.

After the institution of the International Labor Organization, the Czechoslovak Government, and particularly the Ministry of Social Welfare, displayed continuing activity in submitting the Draft Conventions and Recommendations of the International Labor Conferences to the National Assembly, and in drafting and introducing bills to bring existing legislation into conformity with these Conventions and Recommendations. The results were very successful in some fields, but in others, so much opposition was encountered that no action has been taken. To date (June, 1938), Czechoslovakia has ratified and taken appropriate measures to live up to thirteen Conventions.[2] No action was considered necessary on the numerous maritime Conventions, as they do not apply to inland countries like Czechoslovakia. It is of interest to compare Czechoslovakia's record with that of other small European countries which have the following ratifications exclusive of maritime Conventions, to their credit: Belgium 20, Bulgaria 21, Denmark 10, Estonia 14, Finland 12, Greece 12, Hungary 15, Ireland 19, Latvia 12, the Netherlands 15, Norway 14, Poland 13, Rumania 12, Sweden 14, Switzerland 9, and Yugoslavia 14.[3]

On September 4, 1920, the Czechoslovak Government submitted to the National Assembly a motion for the ratification of the Washington Conventions concerning the limitation of the hours of work in industrial establishments to eight in the day and forty-eight in the week, the employment of women during the night, and the minimum age for admission of children to industrial employment. In November, 1920, these three Conventions were presented to the Chamber of Deputies, in accordance with the procedure adopted by Czechoslovakia in the matter of ratifications. They were next given to the Committee on Political and Social and Foreign Affairs of the Senate. As these three Conventions did not entail any modification in existing legislation, which was already in advance of them, they were ratified after brief consideration, and their ratification was registered with the Secretary-General of the League of Nations on August 24, 1921.[4]

The ratification of the other three Conventions adopted by the Washington Conference was delayed because changes had to be made in the existing Czechoslovak legislation. They were laid before the National Assembly in November, 1920, and the following measures were taken in regard to them. To bring the legislation of Czechoslovakia up to the standards of the Convention concerning unemployment, the government, on January 11, 1921, introduced into the National Assembly a bill concerning the organization of labor exchanges and insurance against unemployment. This bill provided for the extension to the whole country of the system of labor exchanges existing in Bohemia, and the establishment of the Ghent system of subsidizing trade union benefits to the unemployed. The bill met with opposition from the Ministry of Agriculture, which desired that the supervision of employment agencies for agricultural laborers should be placed under its charge, while the Ministry of Social Welfare was in favor of a uniform organization for all classes of workers.

The bill, as finally passed, on July 17, 1921, provided that the State should add its contribution to the benefits paid by trade unions to their unemployed members. This State contribution was to be equal to the amount of the benefit paid from the funds of the organization, and the total benefit paid to an unemployed worker might not exceed two-thirds of the normal wage earned when last employed. It was therefore based on the Ghent system.

The provisions of the act gave effect to Paragraph III of the Washington Recommendation concerning unemployment [5] which recommended that each member of the I.L.O. establish an effective system of unemployment insurance, either through a Government system or through a system of Government subventions to associations whose rules provide for the payment of benefits to their unemployed members. Paragraph (2) of Section 1 of the Act of July 19, 1921,[6] facilitated the application of Article 3 of the Convention concerning unemployment. It stated as follows:

"Foreign workers may receive the supplementary State contribution to unemployment benefits on the same terms as the citizens of Czechoslovakia, provided that the State to which such workers belong grants the same privileges to citizens of Czechoslovakia, adopting, where it has not already done so, the necessary legislation, and treating them in this matter on a footing of equality with its own nationals."

There was, however, no provision for changing the existing legislation regarding employment agencies. Therefore, Czechoslovakia was not in a position to ratify the Convention concerning unemployment, Article 2 of which states that "each Member which ratifies this Convention shall establish a system of free public employment agencies under the control of a central authority. Where both public and private free employment agencies exist, steps shall be taken to coordinate the operations of such agencies on a national scale." [7]

In January, 1922, a bill providing for the amendment of the legislation concerning employment exchanges was introduced into the National Assembly. Again in 1930, a bill relating to public employment exchanges was drafted by the Ministry of Social Welfare and circulated to all the Ministries and Government Departments on January 18, 1931, in accordance with the Czechoslovak procedure of interdepartmental discussion. Neither of these bills was enacted into law, however, and Czechoslovakia has not yet (June 1938) ratified the Unemployment Convention.

A Legislative Decree of April 20, 1934 provided for Government control of dismissals and suspensions of work, and required a longer period of notice varying according to length of service.[8] A further Legislative Decree of July 9, 1936 provided that at least one public employment exchange should be set up in each primary administrative area, and that an adequate number of vocational guidance offices should be set up and attached to the larger exchanges.[9]

The ratification of the Convention concerning the employment of women before and after childbirth, also adopted at the Washington Conference, necessitated modifications in two existing acts, the Sickness Insurance Act and the Eight-Hour Day Act. Article 3, paragraph (b) states that a "woman shall have the right to leave her work if she produces a medical certificate stating that her confinement will probably take place within six weeks." Paragraph (c) provides that "while she is absent from her work, she shall be paid benefits sufficient for the full and healthy maintenance of herself and her child, provided either out of public funds or by means of a system of insurance, the exact amount of which shall be determined by the competent authority in each country, and as an additional benefit, shall be entitled to free attendance by a doctor or certified midwife." [10]

By the Sickness Insurance Act, the employment of women was prohibited only for the six weeks after childbirth. It was left to the discretion of the Sickness Benefit Institutions to make special provisions for women before confinement.

The Minister of Social Welfare placed before the National Assembly a number of new provisions intended to modify the existing system, as follows: [11]

(a) Women working in establishments to which the Law of December 19, 1918 applies, may not be employed in ordinary paid work during the six weeks following childbirth.

(b) A pregnant woman who proves by a medical certificate that childbirth will take place in all likelihood within six weeks, may absent herself from her employment unless this latter be of a seasonal character.

(c) An employer may not dismiss a child-bearing woman during the periods mentioned in the preceding paragraphs; nor may he dismiss a woman who proves by a medical certificate that she is suffering from illness as the result of her pregnancy or of childbirth, and that she is in consequence unable to recommence her work.

(d) A woman employed in an establishment to which the Law of December 19, 1918 applies, shall have the right to two rest periods of half an hour during which she may nurse her child.

The last provision necessitated a change in the Eight-Hour Day Law which states in paragraph 3 (2), "at least a quarter of an hour's break must be allowed after not more than five hours' uninterrupted work. These breaks in work need not be allowed to workers over eighteen years of age, provided that a proper period of rest is ensured to them in the regular course of the manufacturing process."

A communication to the I.L.O. in 1921 conveyed the information that final adoption of this bill appeared to be certain. It said that the delay in passing it was due solely to the fact that the Socialist party desired that women employed in agriculture as well as those employed in industry and commerce, should be covered by these measures.[12]

In spite of pressure from the Government, this bill was not enacted into law, and there is no record of any later action being taken on the subject. Czechoslovakia has not ratified the Convention.

Ratification of the Convention which fixed the minimum age for employment of children by night at eighteen years, made it necessary to change existing Czechoslovak legislation which fixed the age limit at sixteen years. The Government drafted a bill prohibiting the night work of young persons under the age of eighteen, but consulted the organization concerned before introducing it into the National Assembly. The Czechoslovak employers requested certain exceptions not provided for in the Convention. These exceptions concerned the night work of young persons in the enamel and porcelain trade, and in coal mines. The employers were willing to withdraw their objections to the first of these, if they could be assured that other countries, especially Germany, would adopt this Convention. More importance was attached by the Government to the second objection. An inquiry was sent to the I.L.O. as to whether, in virtue of the provisions of Article 7 of the Convention, which allow the prohibition of night work to be suspended " when in cases of serious emergency, the public interests demands it ",[13] Czechoslovakia could be authorized, while adhering to the Convention, to suspend its application to coal mines temporarily.

The bill prohibiting the night work of young persons under eighteen years was laid before the Chamber of Deputies in 1921. The demand of the Socialist Party, that the exceptions provided for in the bill should be limited to those enumerated in Article 2 of the Convention, met with considerable opposition. Article 2 states that: "Young persons over 16 may be employed during the night in the following industrial undertakings on work which, by reason of the nature of the process, is required to be carried on continuously day and night:

(a) manufacture of iron and steel;
(b) glass works;
(c) manufacture of paper;
(d) manufacture of raw sugar;
(e) gold mining reduction work"

The records do not show that this bill was enacted into law or that any later action was taken on the subject. Czechoslovakia has not ratified the Convention.

With regard to the Conventions and Recommendations adopted by the International Labor Conference at its second session in Genoa, 1920, Czechoslovakia sent a statement to the I.L.O. that it intended to give effect to them when there were any Czech workers to whom their provisions applied. These Conventions and Recommendations dealt with various phases of the question of employment at sea.

In a letter of March 17, 1923,[14] the Czechoslovak Ministry of Social Welfare informed the I.L.O. that it proposed to deal with the Conventions adopted by the third session at Geneva in 1921 in two groups, as follows:

1. those Conventions, the provisions of which were already carried out by the legislation of Czechoslovakia, and the ratification of which could, therefore, be proceeded with immediately;

2. those Conventions, the execution of which demanded amendments to existing legislation.

With regard to the first group of Conventions, the Ministry of Social Welfare prepared a measure for their ratification, and proposed in agreement with the Ministry of Foreign Affairs, that the Government should submit this measure to the President of the Republic. The Conventions in this group were:

1. Concerning the age for admission of children to employment in agriculture.[15]

The principles of this Convention were considered to be applied by two acts of the Czechoslovak legislature. Section 10 of the Eight-Hour Day Act of December 19, 1918, prohibited the employment of children for wages in the industrial, commercial, transport, and agricultural undertakings defined in Section 1, before they reached the age of fourteen years. The Act of July 17, 1919, relating to the employment of children under fourteen years of age, completely prohibited the employment of children in agriculture until they completed the age of ten years. Children between the ages of ten and fourteen years might be employed in domestic work or on light agricultural work if they lived in the homes of their employers. Nevertheless, it was prohibited on school days to employ children on light work for more than two hours, as two hours before the opening and one hour after the closing of school must be reserved for recreation. During the holidays, other than Sundays and religious festivals for which special provision is made in Section 6, children might not be employed for more than six hours in agriculture and domestic work.

The exceptional arrangements of school hours allowed by Article 2 of the Convention are inadmissible in Czechoslovak law. Article 2 states that " for the purposes of practical vocational instruction the periods and the hours of school attendance may be so arranged as to permit the employment of children on light agricultural work, and in particular, on light work connected with the harvest, provided that such employment shall not reduce the total annual period of school attendance to less than eight months." According to Section 7 of the Act of July 17, 1919, the employment of children under the age of fourteen years is completely prohibited in certain workshops and undertakings enumerated in the Act, and this prohibition may be extended to cases where the conditions of labor are unsuited to the age of the child, or where they might endanger his physical or moral development. The employment of children in brickfields or lime kilns, which may be operated in connection with agricultural undertakings, and in connection with any kind of agricultural machinery is also prohibited. Further extensions of the prohibition of the employment of children are within the competence of the Minister of Social Welfare.

Article 3 of the Convention provides that the prohibition contained in Article 1 shall not apply to work done by children in technical schools, provided that such work is approved and supervised by public authority. The supervision mentioned in this Article is provided for in Section 13 of the Act of July 17, 1919, and is exercised by the local and provincial administrative authorities. The provincial authorities may also set up special supervisory committees for the purpose of providing the authorities with advisory opinions on the application of the law. It is further prescribed that the competent authorities shall be supported by all the other bodies, institutions, or officials concerned with the care of the young.

2. Application of the weekly rest in industrial undertakings.[16]

The Ministry stated that Czechoslovak legislation completely carried out the provisions of this Convention. The Eight-Hour Act of December 19, 1918, provides, in Section 4, for a weekly rest of thirty-two consecutive hours for all wage earners. In undertakings in which production can be interrupted without inconvenience, the weekly rest is ordinarily fixed to fall on Sunday. On the other hand, in undertakings in which work is required to be carried on continuously, a system of rotation is prescribed by which every wage earner shall be able to take his thirty-two hours' rest in such a manner as to include at least one Sunday in every three weeks. In the case of women employed in factories, the weekly rest of thirty-two hours commences on Saturday, not later than 2 p.m.

The provision of Article 2 of the Convention, that the period of rest shall, wherever possible, be granted simultaneously to the whole of the staff of each undertaking, is carried out by Section 2 of the Sunday Rest Act of January 16, 1895, as amended by the Act of July 18, 1905.[17] This Act provided that the Sunday rest shall be simultaneous for all the workers in an undertaking, and the right to grant exceptions in the case of undertakings in which only the members of one single family are employed is restricted by Section 3, paragraph 5, of the Sunday Rest Act, to the personal labor of the employer. Finally, Section 4 and the last paragraphs of Sections 6 and 7 of the Sunday Rest Act fully carry out the provisions of Article 7 of the Convention which provides that each employer shall be obliged:

"(a) where the weekly rest is given to the whole of the staff collectively, to make known such days and hours of collective rest by means of notices posted conspicuously in the establishment or any other convenient place, or in any other manner approved by the Government; (b) where the rest period is not granted to the whole of the staff collectively, to make known by means of a roster drawn up in accordance with the method approved by the legislation of the country, or by a regulation of the competent authority, the workers or employees subject to a special system of rest, and to indicate that system."

3. Rights of association and combination of agricultural workers.

The Ministry stated that the terms of this Convention[18] were fully carried out by the Constitution of the Czechoslovak Republic which guarantees the same rights of association and combination to agricultural as to industrial workers. In Section V, Article 114, paragraph 1, of the Constitutional Charter of the Czechoslovak Republic, it states that "the right of association to safeguard and ameliorate conditions of employment and economic conditions shall be guaranteed."[19]

These three Conventions, after brief consideration by the National Assembly, were recommended by the Government to the President of the Republic for ratification. Their formal ratification was registered by the Secretary-General of the League of Nations, in conformity with Article 406 of the Treaty of Versailles, on August 31, 1923.

With regard to the use of white lead in painting, certain modifications in the existing regulations, as contained in the Decree of April 15, 1908, were found necessary in order to bring them into conformity with the provisions of the Convention concerning the use of white lead in painting [20] adopted by the third session of the International Labor Conference in Geneva in 1921. A bill was prepared by the Ministry of Social Welfare, providing for the following changes in the Decree of April 15, 1908:

1. The minimum age of employment in painting work involving the use of white lead should be raised from sixteen to eighteen and provision made for the compilation of statistics with regard to lead poisoning, as required by Article 7 of the Convention;

2. Medical examination of the workers every three months must take place in all undertakings employing at least ten workers, and not merely, as previously, in undertakings employing twenty workers, or more;

3. The provinces of Slovakia and Sub-Carpathian Russia, formerly part of the Kingdom of Hungary, in which no legislation on the subject existed, were to be included within the scope of the measure.

The bill was introduced in the Chamber of Deputies on March 20, 1924, and referred to the Social Policy Committee. Mr. Tayerly, Social Democrat, who attended the Conference of 1921 as workers' delegate, as rapporteur of the Social Policy Committee, recommended the bill to the Chamber. He added, however, that in his opinion, the bill was not altogether adequate, in view of the fact that it did not involve complete prohibition of the use of paint containing white lead. Mr. Blazek, Communist, also contended that the bill was only a partial improvement on existing regulations, and did not sufficiently protect the health of the workers. An amendment proposed by the Communist party, prohibiting absolutely the use of paint containing white lead, was rejected. The bill was amended by the Senate on April 25, 1924, and referred back to the Chamber, where it was finally passed. The ratification of the Convention concerning the use of white lead in painting was registered by the Secretary-General of the League of Nations on August 31, 1923.[21]

With regard to fixing the minimum age for the admission of young persons to employment as trimmers and stokers, and the compulsory medical examination of children and young persons employed at sea, the Ministry stated that it was not proposed to recommend to the President of the Republic the ratification of these Conventions until they had been ratified by the maritime States, as they had no practical importance for Czechoslovakia.

As to workmen's compensation in agriculture, the Ministry stated it was not considered possible to recommend this Convention [22] for immediate ratification, as its provisions were not carried out fully by Czechoslovak legislation. The legislation in force was based upon the Workmen's Compensation Act of December 28, 1887, as amended by the Act of April 10, 1919. Section 1, paragraph 4 (2) of this law lays down that the obligation to insure against industrial accidents shall only apply to agricultural, rural, and forestry undertakings in which some kind of power-driven machinery is used as a permanent feature of the working of the undertaking. Moreover, Section 5 of the Act prescribes: "If an agricultural, rural, or forestry undertaking, subject to this Act, uses motive power as a permanent part of its plant in such a way that only a certain number of the workers and employees are exposed to danger resulting from employment in connection with such motive power, the obligation to insure shall be restricted to the persons exposed to this danger." [23]

As Article 1 of the Draft Convention concerning Workmen's Compensation in agriculture states that "each member of the International Labor Organization which ratifies this Convention undertakes to extend to all agricultural wage-earners its laws and regulations which provide for the compensation of workers for personal injury by accident arising out of or in the course of their employment", [24] it was clear that the existing legislation of Czechoslovakia only partly corresponded with the principles contained in the Convention. It was therefore considered impossible to ratify the Convention at that time.

The Minister of Social Welfare, however, stated that the Government intended to proceed to the amendment of the Workmen's Compensation Act by extending it to all agricultural wage earners, but that this could not be done until after the adoption of the legislation concerning social insurance which was then in preparation, and which was intended to complete the system of compulsory insurance of the worker against sickness and industrial accidents by insurance against old-age and invalidity, and by making provision for widows and orphans.

By a letter of June 11, 1923,[25] the Ministry of Social Welfare informed the I.L.O. that the Recommendations adopted by the third session of the International Labor Conference, Geneva, 1921, had been divided into three groups, as follows:

1. Those Recommendations, the requirements of which were fully satisfied by existing legislation; namely, the Recommendations concerning night work of women in agriculture, night work of children and young persons in agriculture, the development of technical agricultural education, the application of the weekly rest in commercial establishments, and social insurance in agriculture;

2. Those Recommendations which it would be possible to apply later, after the adoption of legislation which was then in preparation; namely, the Recommendations concerning the prevention of unemployment in agriculture and the protection before and after childbirth of women wage-earners in agriculture;

3. The Recommendation concerning living-in conditions of agricultural workers, which could not be carried out at that time, because of the continuance of the economic crisis and the shortage of houses.

The Recommendations in the first group were approved by the Council of Ministers on May 17, 1923, and the Minister for Foreign Affairs was requested to notify such approval officially. The letter of June 11, 1933, also contained a detailed statement of the state of Czechoslovak legislation in respect of each of the Recommendations, which may be summarized, as follows:

1. Recommendations concerning night work of women in agriculture.

The night work of women in agriculture is regulated by the Eight Hour Day Act of December 19, 1918, Section 9 of which prohibits generally the employment of women during the night, and the Order of January 11, 1919, made in pursuance of the Eight Hour Day Act, Section V, second paragraph of which grants permission for the employment of women over eighteen years of age between 10 P.M. and 5 A.M. in "agricultural undertakings, vine and fruit culture, for the care of animals and for work relating to the arranging and preparation of agricultural produce and the conveyance of goods to the market, provided that these operations cannot be carried out during the day at all, or not to a sufficient extent." [26]

The Recommendations concerning night work of women in agriculture [27] provided that "the General Conference of the International Labor Organization recommends: That each Member of the International Labor Organization take steps to regulate the employment of women wage earners in agricultural undertakings during the night in such a way as to ensure to them a period of rest compatible with their physical necessities, and consisting of not less than nine hours, which shall, when possible, be consecutive."

2. The Recommendation concerning night work of children and young persons in agriculture.[28]

Paragraph I of the Recommendation provides that "steps be taken to regulate the employment of children under fourteen years of age in agricultural undertakings during the night, in such a way as to ensure to them a period of rest compatible with their physical necessities and consisting of not less than ten consecutive hours." Paragraph II states that "steps be taken to regulate the employment of young persons between the ages of fourteen and eighteen years in agricultural undertakings during the night, in such a way as to ensure to them a period of rest compatible with their physical necessities and consisting of not less than nine consecutive hours."

As regards Paragraph I of the Recommendation, the Act respecting child labor of July 17, 1919,[29] provides that children under fourteen years of age employed in agriculture and domestic work are to be allowed an uninterrupted night's rest of ten hours, which are to fall generally between 8 P.M. and 6 A.M. As far as Paragraph II of the Recommendation is concerned, reference is made to Section 9, Sub-Section (1) of the Eight Hour Day Act, which prohibits the employment of young persons under sixteen years of age during the night. In regard to both the night work Recommendations, it was pointed out in the letter of the Ministry of Social Welfare of June 11, 1923, that night work in agriculture is exceptional in Czechoslovakia because of the climatic conditions in the country.

3. The Recommendation concerning the development of technical agricultural education [30] provides that each Member of the International Labor Organization shall "endeavor to

develop vocational agricultural education, and in particular to make such education available to agricultural wage-earners on the same conditions as to other persons engaged in agriculture." It also recommends that "each Member of the International Labor Organization send a report to the International Labor Office at regular intervals, containing as full information as possible as to the administration of the laws, the sums expended, and the measures taken in order to develop vocational agricultural education."

It was considered that the existing vocational agricultural instruction in Czechoslovakia gave effect to the Recommendation. There were a large number of popular agricultural schools in existence, which offered suitable facilities for vocational instruction to agricultural wage-earners. In 1926, twenty scholarships for winter courses in these state agricultural schools were granted by the Ministry of Agriculture. As a great many applied for these scholarships in the first year, the Ministry made arrangements with local bodies to secure the establishment of two local schools in each assizes district.

In 1927 there were 126 special agricultural schools. These schools provide two consecutive years' courses of six months each, the students residing at the schools and giving their whole time to the work. It was estimated that the cost of each student was 2000 crowns a year, so that the total amount could easily be covered by budget economies. The effect was to greatly increase the opportunities of the employed agricultural worker for acquiring vocational education in agriculture.

At the beginning of 1926, the Council set up by the Ministry of Agriculture to establish relations with the national agricultural organization, appointed a special committee in Prague for the purpose of providing the agricultural population with systematic information and instruction by means of wireless telephony. The Committee collects all information of interest to agriculturists, economic, commercial, financial, and cooperative, and broadcasts it twice a day. Arrangements are made to include in the program once a month information on agricultural topics supplied by the agricultural service of the International Labor Office.

In 1925, an Academy of Agriculture was set up in Prague. Its main purpose is to carry on research work and give aids to research work, such as the creation of a library. It also undertakes practical steps toward a solution of agricultural problems. It addresses the competent Ministers on various questions and undertakes inquiries and investigations on its own responsibility. The Academy is in active relationship with the International Labor Office.[31]

4. The Recommendation concerning the application of the weekly rest in commercial establishments,[32] in Paragraph I states "the whole of the staff employed in any commercial establishments, public or private, or in any branch thereof, except as otherwise provided for by the following paragraphs, should enjoy in every period of seven days a period of rest comprising at least twenty-four consecutive hours." This period of rest should, wherever possible, be simultaneous for the whole staff of each establishment, and should be fixed so as to coincide with the days already established by the customs of the country. Paragraph II recommends that each Member take the steps necessary to define any exceptions which may be considered necessary and to draw up a list of such exceptions. Paragraph III recommends that each Member communicate to the International Labor Office the list of the exceptions made in pursuance of Paragraph II, and thereafter, every two years, any modifications of this list.

Section 4, Sub-Section (1) of the Eight Hour Day Act stipulates that each worker is to be allowed a rest period of thirty-two consecutive hours in each week. The provision that the period of rest shall, wherever possible, be granted simultaneously to the whole staff of each establishment is carried out by Section 4, Sub-Section (2) of the Eight Hour Day Act, by Section 1 and Section 2 of the Sunday Rest Act of July 18, 1905, which amended the Act of January 16, 1895;

and for Slovakia and Carpathian Ruthenia, by the Act No. XIII of 1891. Authorization for certain exceptions in the case of commercial establishments is provided for by Sections 3, 6, 9, and 10 of the Act of July 18, 1905, and for Slovakia and Carpathian Ruthenia by Section 1, Sub-Sections 2-5 of the Act No. XIII of 1891.

5. The Recommendation concerning social insurance in Agriculture[33] provided that "each Member extend its laws and regulations establishing systems of insurance against sickness, invalidity, old age, and other similar social risks to agricultural wage-earners on conditions equivalent to those prevailing in the case of workers in industrial and commercial occupations."

The Sickness Insurance Act of October 9, 1924, as amended by the Act of November 8, 1928, applies to every person who performs work or renders services under a contract of employment, service, or apprenticeship. Agricultural workers, therefore, are eligible for the same sickness insurance benefits as industrial workers or employees whose work or apprenticeship is not of a temporary or supplementary character. Old-age insurance is also regulated by the Act of October 9, 1924, as amended by the Act of November 8, 1928.[34]

The Act of December 28, 1887, amended by the Act of April 10, 1919, provides for accident insurance.[35] By virtue of Section 1, Sub-Section (4), Paragraph 2, this Act applies to all agricultural workers employed in agricultural or forestry undertakings in which mechanical appliances are used, whether worked by steam, gas, electricity, wind, water power, or beasts of burden. Sub-Section (4) of Section 1 of this Act further provides that agricultural workers are to be treated in respect of accident insurance on the same footing as industrial workers. Sub-Section (5), however, restricts the responsibility to effect insurance to workers who are directly exposed to danger as a result of the performance of duties in connection with the motor power used in the undertaking.

In regard to Slovakia and to Carpathian Ruthenia, Acts No. XVI of 1900, XIV of 1904, VIII of 1912, and XX of 1913 provide that all farm servants are to be insured against accidents occurring in the course of work in connection with machinery whether power-driven or otherwise.

6. The Recommendation concerning the prevention of unemployment in agriculture,[36] provided that each Member should consider measures for the prevention of unemployment among agricultural workers suitable to the economic and agricultural conditions of its country, and that it should examine particularly, from this point of view, the advisability:

" (1) of adopting modern technical methods to bring into cultivation land which is at present not worked or only partially developed, but which could by such means be made to yield an adequate return;

" (2) of providing facilities for settlement on the land;

" (4) of taking steps to render work of a temporary nature accessible to unemployed agricultural workers by means of the provision of transport facilities;

" (5) of developing industries and supplementary forms of employment which would provide occupation for agricultural workers who suffer from seasonal unemployment, provided that steps be taken to ensure that such work is carried on under equitable conditions;

" (6) of taking steps to encourage the creation of agricultural workers' cooperative societies for the working and purchase or renting of land, and of taking steps to this end to increase agricultural credit, especially in favor of cooperative agricultural associations of land workers established for the purpose of agricultural production.

At that time, legislation regarding this subject was embodied in the Act of July 19, 1921, dealing with State contributions to unemployment insurance funds. This law was later supplemented by the Act of June 5, 1930. A bill regarding the regulation of public employment exchanges was drafted by the

Minister of Social Welfare, and circulated to all the Ministries and Government Departments on January 18, 1931. This bill was not enacted into law, and no action has been taken on this Recommendation.[37]

7. Recommendation concerning the protection before and after childbirth of women wage-earners in agriculture.[38] This Recommendation provides that each Member take measures to ensure to women wage-earners employed in agricultural undertakings, protection before and after childbirth similar to that provided by the Convention adopted by the International Labor Conference at Washington, for women employed in industry and commerce, and that such measures should include the right to a period of absence from work before and after childbirth and to a grant of benefit during the said period, provided either out of public funds or by means of a system of insurance.

The Sickness Insurance Act stipulates that insured women are to receive, during a period of six weeks before and six weeks after childbirth, benefits equivalent to the amount of sickness benefit payable under the Act, provided that they are not in receipt of wages during this period. In 1922, a bill was drafted by the Ministry of Social Welfare, providing the right of women wage-earners to a period of absence six weeks before, as well as six weeks after childbirth. It, however, applies only to women employed in industry and transport undertakings, and not to women in agriculture. For this reason, it failed to become a law, and consequently Czechoslovakia has been unable to ratify the Washington Childbirth Convention, or take any action on this Recommendation.[39]

8. The Recommendation concerning living-in conditions of agricultural workers [40] stated that each Member should " take statutory or other measures to regulate the living-in conditions of agricultural workers with due regard to the special climatic or other conditions affecting agricultural work in its country, and after consultation with the employers' and workers' organ-

izations concerned." It recommended in Paragraph III, that these measures should contain the following provisions:

"(a) unless climatic conditions render heating superfluous, the accommodation intended for workers' families, groups of workers, or individual workers should contain rooms which can be heated.

"(b) accommodation intended for groups of workers shall include a separate bed for each worker, shall afford facilities for ensuring personal cleanliness, and shall provide for the separation of the sexes. In the case of families, adequate provision shall be made for the children.

"(c) stables, cowhouses, and open sheds should not be used for sleeping quarters."

On account of the economic crises and of the housing shortage in Czechoslovakia, it was considered impossible to take any action on this Recommendation. Action on it was postponed until the economic situation became more favorable. Nothing has been done along this line up to the present time, June, 1938.

In a letter of November 2, 1925,[41] the Secretary-General of the League of Nations forwarded to the International Labor Office a copy of a communication dated August 27, 1923, from the Permanent Delegate of the Czechoslovak Republic to the League of Nations. In this communication it was stated that, since Czechoslovak legislation at that time in force was in complete accordance with the requirement of the Recommendations concerning night work of women in agriculture, night work of children and young persons in agriculture, the development of technical agricultural education, the application of the weekly rest in commercial establishments, and social insurance in agriculture, the Council of Ministers has noted and approved them. A statement of the legislative measures giving effect to these Recommendations was communicated to the Director of the International Labor Office by a letter from the Ministry of Social Welfare, dated June 6, 1923.

In a letter of February 9, 1925, the Government of the Czechoslovak Republic informed the I.L.O. that measures had been taken by the Minister of Social Welfare, in agreement with the central factory inspection department and the Minister of Public Hygiene and Physical Culture, for the approval by the Cabinet of the Recommendation concerning the prevention of anthrax, the protection of women and children against lead poisoning, and the establishment of Government health services, all of which were adopted at the Washington Conference in 1919.

At a meeting of February 7, 1925, the Cabinet approved the Recommendation concerning communication to the I.L.O. of statistical and other information regarding emigration, immigration, and the repatriation and transit of emigrants, adopted at the fourth session in Geneva in 1922.

Further, the Minister of Social Welfare took steps at the beginning of January, 1925, for the adoption by the Cabinet of the Recommendation concerning the general principles for the organization of systems of inspection to secure the enforcement of the laws and regulations for the protection of the workers, adopted by the International Labor Conference at its fifth session, Geneva, in 1923. On February 13, 1925,[42] he submitted the Recommendation to the Council of Ministers, as being the competent authority, under Article 405, paragraph 5, of the Treaty of Versailles.

In a letter of September 3, 1925, the Government of Czechoslovakia informed the I.L.O. that, on July 25, 1925, the Council of Ministers approved this Recommendation.[43] The letter included an outline of existing legislation, namely, the Act of June 17, 1883, of the Imperial Code, concerning inspectors of industry which was still valid in Bohemia, Moravia, and Silesia, and Chapter II of Act No. XXVIII of 1893 of the former Kingdom of Hungary, which was still valid in Slovakia and Sub-Carpathian Russia, as amended by Act No. 47 of January 27, 1921.

According to this legislation, supervision by the inspectors extends not only to factories and workshops properly so-called, but also to small industrial undertakings and commercial establishments, whatever the number of persons employed, and irrespective of whether such undertakings use mechanical power. In Slovakia and Sub-Carpathian Russia, in accordance with Paragraph 16 of Chapter II of the Act of 1893, inspection of industries applies also to industrial undertakings connected with agriculture and forestry, and with the production of butter, milk, cheese, and silk.

In view of the fact that the field of application of these provisions corresponds, on the whole, to the scope of the Recommendation of 1923, the Government thought it desirable to adopt the general principles laid down in that Recommendation.[44]

In 1926 and 1927, there was considerable complaint on the part of the workers that the passage of social legislation was not proceeding rapidly enough. The Government's standpoint may be seen in the following excerpt from a speech by the Prime Minister, Mr. Svehla, December 5, 1926, on social policy:[45]

"The policy of the Government must be based on prudence, care being taken that the bounds of economic possibilities are not overstepped. Social reforms would become nugatory if the cost were not covered by output which must create the necessary revenue. Only by this means can social legislation be maintained and developed. If progress is to be made in this direction, and existing legislation is to be fully applied, the proper working of industrial undertakings and the development of production must be guaranteed. Having regard to the fact that capacity to pay is the principal factor to be considered in the collection of funds for the carrying out of social measures, it is the duty of the Government to see that our industries are able to proceed on a sound footing."

The Czechoslovak Federation of National Socialist Unions, which comprises unions of railwaymen, postal employees, textile workers, metal workers, building workers, chemical workers, agricultural workers, salaried employees, and public servants, at its Annual Congress in Prague, April 16-19, 1927, adopted a program of claims including: legislation providing for the relief of workers over 65, reform of accident insurance and its extension to agricultural workers, labor courts, and sickness insurance and pensions for salaried employees. A resolution was adopted by this Congress, stating that:

"The Federation of National Socialist Unions will continue to give energetic support to the efforts of the I.L.O. for the establishment of social justice, and expresses the wish that the Government of the Czechoslovak Republic, appreciating all that the I.L.O. and its Director have done for Czechoslovakia and its workers, will not delay the ratification of the Conventions of the International Labor Organization." [46]

The amalgamation of the Federation of Czechoslovak Trade Unions and the Federation of German Trade Unions in Czechoslovakia, adopted a manifesto in February, 1927, containing the economic and social demands of the Czechoslovak workers. These demands included: support by the Government for the League of Nations proposal for free international exchange, a share in the management of production and the amendment of the acts relating to works councils, the introduction of a bill concerning employment exchanges, revision of the unemployment insurance act, and ratification of the Conventions adopted by the International Labor Conferences, especially the Convention concerning night work in bakeries.

The Workers' Delegate of Czechoslovakia to the tenth session of the International Labor Conference, Mr. Tucny, communicated to the I.L.O. the text of a speech which he had intended to make during the debate on the second part of the Report of the Director. He was unable to make this speech because the debate was clotured. He said, in part, that the workers regretted that Czechoslovakia had allowed herself to be outstripped by other States in the matter of ratifications. Even if it were admitted that the eight Conventions ratified by the Czechoslovak Government were of great importance, the workers of the country insisted that the Government should do still more. On the subject of the Hours Convention, he explained the reasons why Czechoslovak legislation did not follow certain provisions of the Convention, but he pointed out that almost all collective agreements contained the provisions necessary for the strict enforcement of the Convention.

He urged that the Governments should be required not only to reply to all questions asked them concerning the enforcement of Conventions, but to give satisfactory and accurate replies. In his opinion, an explanation such as that given by the Czechoslovak Government to the effect that the increase in overtime hours was due to the development of production, did not correspond with the facts.

He said there was also much to be desired in the enforcement of the Convention prohibiting the night work of women, and of the Convention concerning the minimum age for admission of children to industrial employment. He, therefore, urged the I. L. O. to extend the scope of its inquiries and also to give attention to the question of sanctions. He recommended, further, that attention should be given to the various national courts, the duty of which it was to supervise the enforcement of ratified Conventions. In this way, he thought that the Conference would have at its disposal such information as would allow it to note measures to be taken and reforms to be effected.

In conclusion, Mr. Tucny expressed the hope that Czechoslovakia would be able to maintain the Eight Hour Day, but urged the Office to make a further effort to secure the unconditional ratification of the Hours Convention, by the Members of the International Labor Organization.[47]

The Foreign Affairs Committee of the Czechoslovak Chamber of Deputies discussed on November 16, 1927, a bill submitted in June by Mr. Winter, former Minister of Social Welfare, which provided for hastening the discussion in Parliament of a number of International Labor Conventions which had not yet been ratified by Czechoslovakia. These were, besides the Conventions relating to maritime labor or emigration, adopted at Genoa in 1920 and at Geneva in 1921 and 1926, the Conventions relating to unemployment, childbirth, night work of young persons, adopted at Washington in 1919, workmen's compensation in agriculture, Geneva, 1921, and the Conventions relating to sickness insurance, adopted in 1927.

The bill requested the Government to submit to the Chamber within two months, those Conventions adopted by the International Labor Conference which had not been brought before the competent authority for approval. Mr. Winter stated before the Committee that in his opinion there was no reason why Czechoslovakia should be behind in the general progress of ratifications, especially in view of the fact that the Conventions not yet ratified did not have as much importance from the economic point of view as those already ratified by Czechoslovakia, particularly the Convention relating to hours of work.

On behalf of the Parliamentary majority, Mr. Kramer submitted to the committee an amendment to Mr. Winter's bill, requesting the Government to hasten the preparatory work necessary to enable the Conventions not yet ratified to be submitted to the Chamber as soon as possible. Mr. Kramer emphacized the fact that Czechoslovakia had already ratified the most important laws, and that as regards the other Conventions, discussion was proceeding between Ministries, the Ministry of Social Welfare having communicated these Conventions to the other competent authorities.[48]

In a letter of December 11, 1926, the Minister of Social Welfare informed the I.L.O. of the various measures taken in Czechoslovakia with regard to the decisions of the seventh session of the Conference in Geneva, 1925. The Convention and the Recommendation concerning equality of treatment for national and foreign workers as regards workmen's compensation for accidents [49] had been submitted to the Council of Ministers for ratification, and appropriate action. It was stated that no amendment of existing legislation would be necessary to give effect to them.

As regards the Conventions concerning workmen's compensation for accidents and for occupational diseases, it was stated that their scope exceeded that of existing legislation in Czechoslovakia, but that the Ministry of Social Welfare was then engaged in revising the legislation on accident insurance. It was considered that this revision should render possible the ratification of these two Conventions as well as the adoption of the two Recommendations dealing with the same subject.

The Director of the I.L.O. made a visit to Czechoslovakia, July 1 through July 5, 1927. Although the primary object of the visit was to attend the second workers' Olympiad, the Director discussed with the Minister of Social Welfare and officials of his department the position of Czechoslovakia as regards ratification of Conventions. At that time, Czechoslovakia had ratified eight Conventions. The Director, in his report to the Governing Body, of October, 1927, stated that it was hardly possible to ask Czechoslovakia to ratify the seven maritime Conventions. The question of night work in bakeries and night work of young persons gave rise to difficulties which did not appear easy to overcome at that time.

He went on to state in his report to the Governing Body that a new bill on social insurance was to be discussed either at the end of the year or early in 1928. If it was passed, it was hoped that the ratification of the Conventions on maternity and workmen's compensation for accidents and occupational diseases might be possible.[50]

On his visit, the Director also renewed contact with the various trade union organizations which collaborate in the work of the office: the Czech and German Social Democrat Organization, the National Socialist Organization, and the Christian Trade Union Organization. The Czechoslovak workers at that time had, and still have, strong trade unions, all of which are attached to political parties. Fusion or concentration of the various elements is always a difficult matter.

In 1929, there were in Czechoslovakia 608 trade union organizations of workers, including salaried employees, with a membership of 1,714,991. Of these, 351 unions belonged to 15 national federations, 173 were wholly or mainly composed of manual workers, and 435 of salaried employees and public servants.[51] The largest federation is the Federation of Czechoslovak Trade Unions. Their annual report submitted to the ninth Congress of the Federation held in Prague, September 21-24, 1930, concluded with an appeal to the Ministry of Social Welfare for speedier ratification of the International Labor Conventions.[52] The Congress of Salaried Employees in Czechoslovakia, which held a meeting of their National Association, July 7-9, 1930, submitted a draft economic resolution drawing attention to the importance of economic democracy and criticizing the failure to put into practice the principles laid down by the Geneva Conferences. They adopted a program of demands, concluding with the demand for the development of international social policy and cooperation with the I.L.O.

In April, 1930, the Ministry of Social Welfare drafted a bill relating to workmen's compensation for occupational diseases, and submitted to experts and to the trades concerned for their opinion.

According to the preamble of the bill, insurance against accident should be applied to the occupational diseases included in an accompanying schedule which could be enlarged, if necessary. The schedule included the following diseases: lead poisoning, mercury poisoning, poisoning due to phosphorus, manganese, benzene, carbon monoxide, carbon disulphide, cyanogen and its derivatives, etc.; anthrax; infections of workers in hospitals, scientific laboratories, etc.; glanders; affections due to radiation, electricity, X-rays; silicosis and siderosis; pneumonia due to Thomas slag; skin diseases caused by exotic woods, soot, paraffin, tar, etc.; glassworkers' cataract; deafness; occupational neuritis, etc.

It was not then decided whether the question of compensation for occupational diseases would be dealt with in a special act, or whether the Accident Insurance Act would be amended. Reference was made in the press, in connection with the bill, to the International Labor Convention concerning workmen's compensation for occupational diseases, adopted in 1925.

In July, 1931, the Minister of Social Welfare informed the I.L.O. that he had proposed to his Government the ratification of the Convention concerning workmen's compensation for occupational diseases, and that a bill to give effect to the Convention had been drafted and submitted to all Government Departments on July 8, 1931, for the usual inter-departmental examination.

On April 22, 1932, the Czechoslovak Cabinet approved the bill relating to compensation for occupational diseases, and the proposal of the Minister of Social Welfare for the ratification of the International Labor Convention concerning workmen's compensation for occupational diseases. The bill was then introduced into the Senate and Chamber of Deputies where it was enacted into law, going into effect on July 1, 1932. It provided that the Act of December 28, 1887, respecting workers' accident insurance, Act No. XIX of 1907 respecting sickness and accident insurance for persons employed in industry and commerce, Act No. XVI of 1900 respecting the relief fund for agricultural laborers and servants, and the provisions of the legislative measures to supplement and amend these acts, shall apply to occupational diseases. These include diseases caused by lead, phosphorus, mercury, arsenic, mangenese, and their compounds, benzene and allied substances, and nitro and amido derivatives of the aromatic series; sulphuretted hydrogen, military gases such as phosgene, thio, etc.; carbon monoxide, hydrocyanic acid and its derivatives; diseases caused by the prolonged action of X-rays, radium, or radio-activity; serious and incurable eczema or cancer caused by soot, paraffin, tar, creosote, anthracene, pitch, or similar substances and its sequelae; cancer of the lungs caused by radio-activity; anthrax; infectious diseases; glanders, diseases of the muscles, bones, or joints of workers employed on drills, hammers, pneumatic riveters, and similar machines, ankylostomiasis; diseases of the respiratory passages caused by the action of basic slag; serious pneumoconiosis due to quartz dust or iron ore dust; diseases due to chromium compounds; serious cataract, and the serious and complex form of nystagmus. It was provided that the list may be amended and supplemented by Government Order. The act also provided for compulsory notification of these diseases.[53]

On September 19, 1932, the Secretariat of the League of Nations registered the ratification of the Convention concerning workmen's compensation for occupational diseases by the Czechoslovak Government.[54]

In a letter of January 10, 1933, the permanent delegate of the Czechoslovak Republic accredited to the League of Nations informed the Secretary-General, in accordance with Article 405 of the Treaty of Versailles, that his Government, on April 24, 1932, had approved the Recommendation concerning workmen's compensation for occupational diseases.[55]

In January, 1935, the Minister of Social Welfare circulated to the other Departments a draft bill for the purpose of excluding women and young persons under eighteen years of age from employment in certain processes in the treatment and handling of lead and zinc. It also laid down certain conditions to be observed in regard to the employment of adult male workers in such processes. The operations from which women and young persons under eighteen were excluded were those enumerated in the Lead Poisoning (Women and Children) Recommendation, 1919,[56] and the restrictions to be imposed relative to the employment of adult male workers in these processes were those prescribed in the Recommendation for women and young persons where their employment is permitted in processes involving the use of lead compounds, with the addition of more detailed requirements as to the state of the workrooms, lighting, and ventilation, methods of cleaning, and protective clothing. The bill also provided for medical examination upon the engagement of employees, and the rejection of the unfit.[57]

The formal ratification by Czechoslovakia of the Convention concerning equality of treatment of national and foreign workers as regards workmen's compensation for accidents, adopted by the seventh session at Geneva in 1925, was registered by the Secretariat of the League of Nations on February 8, 1927.[58] By letter of June 2, 1928, the Permanent Delegate of Czechoslovakia to the League informed the Secretary-General that his Government had adopted the Recommendation on the same subject.[59] A treaty providing for reciprocity of treatment of foreign workers carrying out the terms of the Recommendation had been signed by Czechoslovakia and France on March 20, 1920.[60] The Recommendation, in Article I, states that, in order to facilitate the application of the Convention concerning equality of treatment for national and foreign workers as regards workmen's compensation for accidents, the Conference recommends that:

(a) when a person to whom compensation is due under the laws and regulations of one member resides in the territory of another member, the necessary measures be taken to facilitate the payment of such compensation and to ensure the observance of the conditions governing such payment laid down by the said laws and regulations;

(b) in case of dispute concerning the non-payment, cessation of payment, or reduction of the compensation due to a person residing elsewhere than in the territory of the member where his claim to compensation originated, facilities be afforded for taking proceedings in the competent courts of law in such territory without requiring the attendance of the persons concerned;

(c) any advantage in respect of exemption from duties and taxes, free issue of official documents, or other privileges granted by the law of any Member for purposes connected with workmen's compensation be extended under the same conditions to the nationals of the other members which shall have ratified the aforementioned Convention.

The treaty between France and the Czechoslovak Republic provided, in Article I, paragraph 2, that " Immigrant workers shall receive for equal work remuneration equal to that of nationals in the same occupation and of the same degree of skill employed in the same undertaking, and the said remuneration shall be based on the customary rate of wages current in the district."

Paragraph 3 states that " They shall enjoy the protection afforded to workers by the domestic legislation of the high contracting parties, and also any protection which the contracting parties may guarantee them in virtue of special Conventions concluded between themselves or with other Powers.

"As regards occupational accidents, the restrictions provided for in respect of Czechoslovakian workers who are victims of accidents and of their survivors or representatives who (at the time of the accident) were not resident or who have ceased to reside in French territory, shall be entirely repealed, in conformity with Section 3, last paragraph, of the French Act of April 9, 1898, respecting occupational accidents, under the conditions laid down in the said paragraph, in consideration of the reciprocity guaranteed to French workers by Czechoslovakian legislation recognized as equivalent.

" The necessary provisions of the payment of pensions and allowances in France and Czechoslovakia shall be laid down by an agreement concluded in the form of an arrangement between the competent French and Czechoslovakian administrative departments."

Treaties giving effect to the Convention concerning equality of treatment of national and foreign workers as regards workmen's compensation for accidents, were made with Austria and Germany in 1933, with Argentina in 1934, and with Yugoslavia in 1936.[61]

With regard to the question of night work in bakeries in Czechoslovakia, and to the ratification of the International Labor Convention on that subject, there was considerable discussion in Parliament, and among employers and employees, lasting over a period of about five years. In Article 8 of the Eight Hour Day Act of December 19, 1918, night work is forbidden between 10 P.M. and 5 A.M. In 1925, the Central Organization of Czechoslovak Chambers of Commerce sent questionnaires to the master bakers' associations in the various districts, referring to the Draft Convention on night work in bakeries, adopted by a provisional vote at the sixth International Labor Conference in 1924, and pointing out that it would allow work to be started at 4 o'clock in the morning. The questionnaire went on to state that most of those concerned demanded that a four o'clock start should be permitted at once, and that total exemption from any prohibition of night work should be granted to the master baker working alone.

The replies to the questionnaire varied greatly. The Federation of Master Bakers Associations of Moravia replied that the regulation of night work in bakeries in force at that time was not satisfactory, as the five o'clock start retarded production, and prevented the sale and consumption of bakery products. They suggested that the appropriate hour for beginning work would be 4 A.M. for the smaller bakeries, and 4:30 for the large mechanical bakeries. They considered, however, that the prohibition of night work should also apply to master bakers working alone.

The Federation of Master Bakers Associations of Bohemia gave a similar reply. They proposed that work should begin at 7 A.M. in the small bakeries, and at 5 A.M. in the large bakeries. On the other hand, the Prague Association of Master Bakers replied that they did not agree that work in bakeries should be permitted to begin at 4 A.M., as public interest and social welfare did not require it. They proposed that work should start at 5 A.M., as that hour met the needs of consumers as well as producers. They did not agree that master bakers working alone, or with members of their families, should be exempted from the prohibition of night work.[62]

On October 28, 1924, the Congress of the Federation of Trade Unions in the Food Trade, while adopting the draft provisionally agreed upon at Geneva as a basis of discussion, nevertheless demanded an interval of eight hours' rest, from 10 P.M. to 6 A.M. A like protest was made by this Federation at Prague on November 14, as a consequence of the report of Mr. Hejna, the workers' technical adviser at the sixth International Labor Conference. The Conference of Bakery Workers of Western Bohemia, held on December 25, 1924, at Plzen, adopted a resolution to the effect that the current regulation of night work must be maintained, and the attacks made by the Central Organization of the Chambers of Commerce must be resolutely repulsed. A similar meeting held at Most by the bakery workers of that district also protested against the action of the Chambers of Commerce.[63]

The Union of Czechoslovakia Master Bakers, basing its request on the provision in the Draft Convention adopted by the International Labor Conference, which allowed work to be begun at 4 A. M., urged the Czechoslovak Government to authorize them to start work at that hour, instead of at 5 A.M. As a reply to this, the Union of Operative Bakers, affiliated with the Federation of Czechoslovak Socialist Trade Unions, met at Prague and decided to do its utmost to preserve the nightly rest period in force at that time. Mr. Stastny, who was the Czechoslovak Workers' Delegate at the fifth session of the International Labor Conference in Geneva in 1923, assured the Bakers' Union of support.

In view of the increase in the number of cases of non-observance of the prohibition of night work and Sunday work in bakeries, and also in view of the various requests for modifications in the regulations, the Minister of Social Welfare decided to open an inquiry into the matter. At this inquiry, a large number of representatives of the employers' and workers' organizations, and also representatives of the Chambers of Commerce and of the administrative departments were present.

The employers' representatives urged the necessity of restricting the statutory rest period during the night and on Sunday, and recommended that work should begin at 4 A.M., 2 A.M., or even 1 A.M. The workers' representatives opposed the arguments of the employers, and called for the maintenance and enforcement of the existing legislation. They also demanded the immediate ratification of the Draft Convention concerning night work in bakeries. After this exchange of views, the Minister of Social Welfare invited the two parties to come to an understanding, and to consider the possibility of finding some solution to the question.

The Central Association of Czechoslovak Chambers of Commerce addressed a memorandum to the Ministries of Commerce, Industry, Social Welfare, and the Interior, in which it endeavored to show the necessity for night work in bakeries, and protested against the provisions of the Geneva Convention on the subject. The memorandum contained the following passages:[64]

It is undeniable that consumers, especially the workers, have need of bread, etc., early in the day, at an hour at which, under present conditions, it is impossible to supply them. The prohibition of night work in bakeries jeopardizes not only large bakeries but also master bakers; the withdrawal of modification of the prohibition of night work would benefit not only consumers and producers, but also working bakers, as it would result in a decrease of unemployment.

The Chambers of Commerce insist on the necessity for the amendment of the regulation of night work in bakeries, and protest that the Geneva Convention does not take into account needs and customs in Czechoslovakia. As regards the text of the Convention, the Chambers of Commerce make the following observations:

The text of paragraph 2 extending the prohibition of night work to employers, is considered unacceptable by the Chamber of Commerce, in view of the fact that the constitutional liberty of a citizen cannot be limited by the prohibition to work whenever he likes.

The Association recalls the fact that cake and pastry-making involves a great deal of time, and that it is not sufficient for work to begin at 5 a. m. It is even too late for work to begin at 4 a. m.

The scope and length of time for preparatory and complementary work should not be regulated in an arbitrary manner, as these depend on the technical equipment of each establishment, seasonal and other circumstances.

The Association also does not accept the exclusion of young persons under 18 from preparatory and complementary work, and demands the inclusion of young persons of 16 years and over.

With regard to temporary exceptions to the prohibition of night work in bakeries, the Association considers that holiday resorts, fairs, etc., should be expressly defined as being covered by such exceptions.

In view of the foregoing, the Central Association of Chambers of Commerce submitted to the Ministries the following claims:

1. That the prohibition of night work for small employers working alone should be repealed, and that an energetic protest should be made against this provision by the Czechoslovak Government representative at the next session of the International Labor Conference.

2. That bakers should be authorized to begin work at 4 A.M., and small bakers in outlying suburbs and small country towns might begin work at 3 A.M.

3. That bakery products should be on sale on Sunday mornings.

4. That the Government should regulate the question with regard to local conditions, and demand the amendment of, or addition to the Geneva Convention, in the light of the above data and claims.

The trade union press stated that the campaign of the Chembers of Commerce against the existing prohibition of night work in bakeries was spreading. Whereas the Association, at first, confined itself to demanding that work should be begun at an earlier hour, it now demanded the permission to work on Sundays, the suppression of the limitation of hours for preparatory and complementary work, the lessening of the protection given by law to young persons, all of which demands the workers entirely opposed.

At the suggestion of the Ministry of Social Welfare, a conference was held on November 18, 1926, under the chairmanship of Mr. Pokorny, Chief Inspector of Labor, to investigate the matter in conjunction with the organizations concerned. At this conference, the employers insisted that work should be permitted to begin before 5 A.M., contending that the requirements of consumers necessitated this. As the trade union representatives opposed this suggestion, the conference was unable to come to any decision, except to appoint a sub-committee of employers' and workers' representatives to go into the question further.

On April 28, 1927, the Minister of Social Welfare convened the Sub-Committee in order to arrive at an understanding. As this proved to be impossible, the Minister of Social Welfare, on May 7, 1927, issued an Order, to come into force immediately, authorizing the beginning of actual work in bakeries at 4 A.M., preparatory and supplementary work being regulated in accordance with the Eight Hour Day Act. The Decree aroused indignant protest from the Socialist press, which anticipated that preparatory work in bakeries would, in fact, begin soon after midnight. The bakers' trade unions organized a twenty-four hours' strike at Prague and Brno on May 13 as a protest, and on the same date convened a meeting at Prague, at which a resolution was unanimously adopted, calling upon the trade union federations and parliamentary groups of socialist deputies to make efforts for the restoration of the former regulations, and instructing the workers' representatives to uphold the same point of view in connection with the forthcoming revision of the collective agreement then in force in the baking trade.

On July 8, 1927, the Social Democratic group of Deputies drew the attention of the Czechoslovak Chamber to a violation of the Eight Hour Day Act, which, it alleged, had been committed by the promulgation of an Order of the Minister of Social Welfare, No. 2580, dated May 7, 1927, authorizing the beginning of actual work in bakeries at 4 A.M. The Order was alleged to be illegal, on the grounds that it was issued without preliminary consultation of the Ministers concerned, that exemptions under the Eight Hour Day Act must be determined by Government Decree, and not by the Order of a single Minister, and finally, that the Order was not published in the Official Gazette, but only in the Official Bulletin of the Ministry of Social Welfare which normally contained only instructions of internal application not affecting the public. It was asked whether the Minister of Social Welfare was prepared to restore the normal working period in accordance with the Eight Hour Day Act and to institute strict supervision of its enforcement in collaboration with representatives of the trade unions.

In reply to these questions, the Minister of Social Welfare stated that the Order of May 7, 1927, was based on Section 8, Paragraph 2, of the Act of December 19, 1918, relating to the Eight Hour Day, which permits the Minister of Social Welfare, in agreement with the other Ministers interested, to take the necessary steps in connection with night work in undertakings where work is not continuous. The Minister added that he was making every effort to ensure that the Eight Hour Day Act be observed as completely as possible in all its provisions, including those relating to the prohibition of night work, and that, as far as possible, this observance was being supervised with the help of representatives of operative bakers.[65]

By a note dated January 21, 1927, the Czechoslovak Minister of Social Welfare presented to the Cabinet, with a view to the initiation of the procedure for ratification, the Convention concerning night work in bakeries, adopted by the seventh session of the International Labor Conference in Geneva in 1925.[66]

On February 27, 1929, the Minister of Social Welfare sent an inquiry to the Director of the I.L.O. as to the meaning of certain terms used in the Convention. He asked for an interpretation of the third sentence of Article 2 which states that " when it is required by the climate or season, or when it is agreed between the employers' and workers' organizations concerned . . . ," and of Paragraph 1 of Article 3, which states " after consultation with the employers' and the workers' organizations concerned, the competent authority in each country may make the following exceptions to the provisions of Article 1." He asked if the employers' and workers' organizations concerned should be considered to be the most important employers' and workers' organizations in the baking industry covering the whole State, or as the employers' and workers' organizations concerned (in the baking industry) operating separately in the various parts of the State. He also asked if the agreement would be considered sufficient if it had been reached between the employers' and workers' organizations concerned, with the opposition of a minority in one or the other of the parties concerned or if the agreement must be unanimous.

The Director replied, on April 11, 1929, that as the Convention did not contain any definition of the employers' and workers' organizations concerned, it was for the Governments to decide, on their own responsibility, which organizations they considered to be those " concerned " in the application of the Convention. To the second question, the Director replied that it would seem that, as in the previous case, the question must be solved in each country by taking the circumstances there into account. He added that in the absence of a contrary provision, the rule seemed to be that decisions are valid if adopted by a majority.[67]

On February 14, 1930, the Czech Minister of Social Welfare called a meeting of the representatives of the employers' and workers' organizations concerned, for the purpose of initiating negotiations in regard to the ratification of the Convention concerning night work in bakeries. The representatives of the workers' organizations urged the ratification of the Convention, but the delegates of the Federation of Chambers of Industry and Commerce were in favor of allowing work to begin at 3 A.M., and the representatives of the food industry were in favor of continuing night work.[68]

No further action has been taken on this subject, the Chart of the Progress of Ratifications, June 1938, showing only that Czechoslovakia has recommended the Convention concerning night work in bakeries to the competent national authority for approval.

On December 13, 1927, the Czechoslovak Government ordered that the instrument of ratification of the Convention concerning the simplification of the inspection of emigrants on board ship,[69] adopted by the eighth session of the International Labor Conference, in Geneva in 1926, should be presented to the President for ratification. Legislation on this subject was already in force, under the terms of the Act respecting Emigration of February 15, 1922.[70] Formal ratification of this Convention by Czechoslovakia was registered by the Secretariat of the League of Nations on May 25, 1928.[71]

At the same time, the Government instructed the Minister of Foreign Affairs to communicate to the Secretary-General of the League of Nations the acceptance of the Recommendation concerning the protection of emigrant women and girls on board ship,[72] also adopted by the eighth session of the International Labor Conference, Geneva, 1926.

In a letter of September 5, 1928,[73] the Minister of Social Welfare of Czechoslovakia informed the I.L.O. that by letter of July 14, 1928, he had submitted to the President of the Council of Ministers and to all the Ministries, the Conventions concerning sickness insurance for workers in industry and commerce and domestic servants, and concerning sickness insurance for agricultural workers, also the Recommendation concerning the general principles of sickness insurance adopted by the tenth session of the International Labor Conference,

1927, with a view to the ratification of the Conventions and the adoption of the Recommendation.

The letter added that the principles of the Conventions and Recommendations were in conformity with the principles of existing Czechoslovak legislation, and in particular with the Act of October 9, 1924, concerning the insurance of employees against sickness, invalidity, and old age.

On October 19, 1928,[74] the Czechoslovak Government approved the Conventions concerning sickness insurance, and submitted them to the President for ratification. Formal ratification of these Conventions by the President was registered by the Secretariat on January 17, 1929.[75] On May 31, 1929,[76] the Czechoslovak Government approved the Recommendation concerning the general principles of sickness insurance adopted by the tenth session, Geneva, 1927. By letter of July 13, 1929,[77] the Permanent Delegate of Czechoslovakia to the League of Nations informed the Secretary-General that his Government had approved the Recommendation concerning the general principles of sickness insurance.

In 1927, an association for the use of workers' spare time was founded in Prague under the auspices of the Czechoslovak Confederation of Labor, a federation of trade unions with a membership of 307,000. The objects of the association were to encourage the good use of workers' spare time, especially of paid annual holidays under the Act of April 3, 1925,[78] from the point of view of health, culture, and social welfare, to organize excursions and travel for purposes of recreation and study, to organize intellectual and physical education, to run organized savings clubs, to form small gardens, and to acquire premises and land suitable for these activities.

By letter of December 31, 1929,[79] the Minister of Social Welfare, in accordance with Paragraph 5 of Article 405 of the Treaty of Versailles, submitted to the Council of Ministers and the competent department and authorities, the Recommendation concerning the development of facilities for the utilization of workers' spare time,[80] adopted by the International

Labor Conference at its sixth session in Geneva in 1924, with a view to taking the necessary steps to accept the Recommendation. On August 20, 1929, the Czechoslovak Government voted to accept the Recommendation and by letter of March 6, 1930,[81] informed the Secretary-General of the League of Nations that it had approved the Recommendation, stating that existing legislation gave full effect to its provisions.

In a letter of February 16, 1929,[82] the Minister of Social Welfare submitted the Convention concerning the creation of minimum-wage fixing machinery and the Recommendation concerning the application of minimum-wage fixing machinery,[83] Geneva, 1928, for preliminary study, to the Ministries of Foreign Affairs and Commerce and Agriculture, to the most representative national trade organization, and to the national Chamber of Commerce.

On November 28, 1929, the Ministry of Social Welfare submitted the Convention and the Recommendation regarding minimum-wage fixing machinery to the Government and to all the Ministries and Departments concerned, with a view to ratification of the Convention and acceptance of the Recommendation. This action was evidently all that was taken in regard to the question of the minimum-wage in Czechoslovakia. The official Chart: Progress of Ratifications, June, 1938 shows that the Convention concerning the creation of minimum-wage fixing machinery has only been recommended to the competent national authority for approval. There is no record that anything further was done in regard to the Recommendation. The reason for this is that the Czechoslovak Government, as well as the employers, oppose the extension of the minimum wage to work other than home work where it has been in force since 1919, by the act regulating working conditions in home industries, of December 12, 1919.[84]

On February 21, 1929, the Minister of Social Welfare submitted the Conventions and Recommendations relating to the protection of persons employed in navigation, adopted by the International Labor Conference at its second (1920), third

(1921), and ninth (1926) sessions, to the Danube, Elbe, and Oder Navigation Companies at Bratislava, Prague, and Vitkovice, respectively.[85]

By letter of November 27, 1930,[86] the Minister of Social Welfare informed the I.L.O. that on November 13, he submitted to the Cabinet, in accordance with Article 405, Paragraph 5, of the Treaty of Versailles, the Conventions adopted by the International Labor Conference at its twelfth session, Geneva, 1929. He also submitted the Recommendations adopted at that session.

Action was taken on one of the Conventions. By letter of December 28, 1933,[87] the Minister of Social Welfare informed the I.L.O. that the Czechoslovak Government unanimously approved, on December 23, 1933, the Convention concerning the marking of weight on heavy packages transported by vessels.[88] A bill, carrying out the provisions of the Convention was at that time under discussion in the National Assembly. This bill was enacted into law on December 18, 1934.[89] Formal ratification of the Convention by the Czechoslovak Government was registered by the Secretariat on March 26, 1934.[90]

The Convention provided that any package or object of 1,000 kilograms (one metric ton) or more gross weight, consigned within the territory of any Member for transport by sea or inland waterway, should have its gross weight plainly and durably marked upon the outside, before being loaded on a ship. The terms of the Act of December 18, 1934, concerning the marking of weight coincide exactly with the provisions of the Convention.

The other Convention and two of the Recommendations adopted by the twelfth session, 1929, concerned the protection against accidents of workers employed in loading and unloading ships. No action has been taken on them due to the fact that the question is of little importance in the inland state of Czechoslovakia. The other two Recommendations had to do with prevention of industrial accidents and responsibility for the protection of power-driven machinery. There is no record of any action having been taken on either of these.

In regard to the question of hours of work, concerning which one Convention and three Recommendations were adopted by the International Labor Conference at its fourteenth session, Geneva, 1930,[91] the Minister of Social Welfare in Czechoslovakia drafted a bill, which, if enacted, would have legalized an even shorter (forty hour) week than the forty-eight hours stipulated in this Convention and in two Recommendations of the 1930 International Labor Conference. The proposal was sent to the various Ministries in 1931 for preliminary examination. A bill containing these provisions was introduced in the Chamber of Deputies by the Social Democratic Party on July 8, 1931, and by the National Socialist Party on July 10, 1931. Both provided for a working week of forty hours; the first included rest periods. In the case of unhealthy, exhausting, or dangerous work, hours should be six in the day and thirty-six in the week. The weekly rest should be at least thirty-six hours. Overtime would have to be paid for at 25 to 100 per cent above normal rates. Exemptions might be granted by Decree under certain conditions for undertakings carrying on continuous processes, if the public interest so required.

There is no record of any action on either bill,[92] the Chart of the Progress of Ratifications of June 1938 showing that legislation on that subject in Czechoslovakia is still in progress or in preparation.

The Convention relating to hours of work in coal [93] mines adopted by the fifteenth session of the International Labor Conference, in 1931, presented special difficulties, not only in Czechoslovakia, but in all of the chief coal-producing countries. Each country feared that the first one which ratified the Convention would be placed at an economic disadvantage.

The Convention in Article 3 (both in Convention No. 31, 1931, and in No. 46, Revised, 1935) states that the "time spent in an underground mine shall mean the period between the time when the worker enters the cage in order to descend and the time when he leaves the cage after re-ascending." It also states that "in no underground hard coal mine shall the time spent in the mine by any worker exceed seven hours and forty-five minutes in the day."

The calculation of the length of the shift is an essential factor in an international regulation of hours of work in mines. The Washington Hours Convention covered mining undertakings, but when this Convention was drafted, in 1919, no special reference was made to the peculiar nature of underground work or to the calculation of the length of the shift. There was therefore the risk that the application of the general provisions of the Washington Convention to mines might lend itself to the adoption of somewhat different régimes.

Regulations adopted in those countries which ratified the Washington Convention indicated that in practice a variety of methods was being used in carrying out its requirements in respect to work in mines. Belgium and Czechoslovakia were the only countries having ratified the Convention in which the method of calculating the length of shifts was legally regulated.

In Czechoslovakia, the Act of December 19, 1918, which applies "to mining undertakings both below ground and on the surface", provides that "the entry and leaving of the mines shall be regarded as a subsidiary operation, provided that the shift shall not be increased thereby by more than half an hour reckoned from the descent of the first workman until the last workman of the same shift leaves the mine." The point is, in practice, covered by collective agreements which include the descent and ascent of the shift in the working day, so that the individual time spent in the mine is under eight hours. If the application of the act were not supplemented by agreements, however, the individual time spent in the mine would be over eight hours.[94]

In 1932, the I.L.O. issued invitations to the Governments of Belgium, Czechoslovakia, France, Germany, England, the

Netherlands, and Poland, to attend a meeting in Geneva to discuss the question of ratification of this Convention. The meeting was held at the I.L.O. on January 7, 1932. The representatives explained the position of the respective Governments in regard to the ratification of the Convention, and drew special attention to the necessity that ratification by the seven Governments represented at the meeting should be simultaneous. In spite of the apparent desire to come to some agreement, no definite results were obtained.[95]

A meeting of the Executive Committee of the International Miners' Federation was held in Geneva on January 8 and 9, 1932, under the chairmanship of Mr. J. Desjardin of Belgium. The committee considered the situation in various countries with reference to the possibility of simultaneous ratification of the Convention limiting hours of work in coal mines. After a long discussion, the Committee unanimously adopted the following Resolution:[96]

"The Executive Committee of the International Miners' Federation notes with indignation, that the Conference of Government representatives of Great Britain, Germany, Poland, France, Belgium, Czechoslovakia, and the Netherlands, which was held in Geneva, on January 7, 1932, with the object of discussing the possibility of ratifying the Convention limiting hours of work in coal mines, has not reached satisfactory conclusions and has adjourned. . . .

"The miners of all countries will receive the news of this postponement with profound disappointment. They had been led to hope that after the protracted and arduous negotiations of the past few years, the Convention of 1931 would have been ratified without further delay.

"The Executive Committee protests with the utmost possible emphasis against the so-called economic arguments which have been advanced by certain governments.

"The Committee addresses an urgent appeal to national affiliated organizations and calls upon them to examine and determine appropriate measures with the object of inducing recalcitrant governments to abandon their attitude, which is disapproved entirely by organized labor."

The records show that no action has been taken by Czechoslovakia on this Convention to date, June, 1938.

Of the sixty-two Conventions adopted by the International Labor Conference from 1919 through 1937, Czechoslovakia has ratified thirteen. They are the following:

No. 1, Hours of Work, adopted in 1919, ratified by Czechoslovakia in 1921.

No. 4, Night Work (Women), adopted in 1919, ratified by Czechoslovakia in 1921.

No. 5, Minimum Age (Industry), adopted in 1919, ratified by Czechoslovakia in 1921.

No. 10, Minimum Age (Agriculture), adopted in 1921, ratified by Czechoslovakia in 1924.

No. 11, Right of Association (Agriculture), adopted in 1921, ratified by Czechoslovakia in 1923.

No. 13, White Lead (Painting), adopted in 1921, ratified by Czechoslovakia in 1923.

No. 14, Weekly Rest (Industry), adopted in 1921, ratified by Czechoslovakia in 1923.

No. 18, Workmen's Compensation (Occupational Diseases), adopted in 1925, ratified by Czechoslovakia in 1932.

No. 19, Equality of Treatment (Accident Compensation), adopted in 1925, ratified by Czechoslovakia in 1927.

No. 21, Inspection of Emigrants, adopted in 1926, ratified by Czechoslovakia in 1928.

No. 24, Sickness Insurance (Industry, etc.), adopted in 1927, ratified by Czechoslovakia in 1929.

No. 25, Sickness Insurance (Agriculture), adopted in 1927, ratified by Czechoslovakia in 1929.

No. 27, Marking of Weight (Packages Transported by Vessels), adopted in 1929, ratified by Czechoslovakia in 1934.

Of the fourteen Conventions adopted by the International Labor Conferences up to 1929 which have not been ratified by Czechoslovakia, seven are concerned with questions of employment at sea, and therefore have little or no application in Czechoslovakia. The other seven which Czechoslovakia has not ratified are as follows:

No. 2, Unemployment, adopted in 1919.
No. 3, Childbirth, adopted in 1919.
No. 6, Night Work (Young Persons), adopted in 1919.
No. 12, Workmen's Compensation (Agriculture), adopted in 1921.
No. 17, Workmen's Compensation (Accidents), adopted in 1925.
No. 20, Night Work (Bakeries), adopted in 1925.
No. 26, Minimum Wage-fixing Machinery, adopted in 1928.

The Chart of the Progress of Ratifications of June 1938 shows that Conventions Nos. 2, 3, 6, 20, 26, 43, and 49 have been recommended to the competent national authority for approval, and that legislation is in progress or in preparation in connection with Conventions Nos. 3, 6, 9, 12, 17, 30, 43, and 49. With regard to the Conventions from No. 28, Protection against Accidents (Dockers), adopted in 1929, through Convention No. 62, Safety Provisions (Building), adopted in 1937, the Chart shows that no action has been taken, except for legislation in progress or preparation in connection with Convention No. 30, Hours of Work (Commerce and Offices), No. 43, Sheet-Glass Works, and No. 49, Reduction of Hours of Work (Glass Bottle Works). As for Recommendations, there is no record in Industrial and Labor Information that action has been taken or urged by the Government on any Recommendation since the one adopted in 1928 concerning Minimum Wage-fixing Machinery.

The reason for this is not that Czechoslovakia has lost faith in the International Labor Organization. Their Minister of

Social Welfare, Mr. Czech, addressing the Budget Committee of the Chamber of Deputies on November 11, 1930,[97] expressed the greatest interest in the work of the I.L.O. and said that the Government of Czechoslovakia was in full agreement with its program. He regretted that he had not been able to obtain ratification of such important Conventions as those relating to night work of children and the employment of women before and after childbirth.

At that time, 1930, work was being done in amending the social insurance program and strengthening the insurance funds. Bills were being drafted concerning workmen's compensation for occupational diseases and accident insurance tribunals. Efforts were being made to open negotiations with Austria and Germany on the question of reciprocity in social insurance matters.

At that time, and continuing to the present, 1938, the attention of the Government of Czechoslovakia was to a considerable extent taken up with the problem of unemployment. At the end of September, 1930, the total number of registered unemployed was 103,860. The actual number of persons totally unemployed was about 300,000, while the number of persons on short time was even greater. This situation called for the expenditure of large sums of money by the Government, and resulted in a decrease in the funds available for developing their program of social legislation.

In 1931, the Czechoslovak Parliament adopted several measures providing for the execution of public works for the purpose of improving the unemployment situation. A national loan of 1,300 million crowns was authorized. Of this sum, 600 millions were allocated to the railways, 150 millions to relief in kind, including the distribution of food and clothing to unemployed persons, the provision of milk for their children, and the purchase of agricultural machinery, and 150 millions to publicly owned undertakings and the Road Fund. Two other acts were adopted, providing respectively for the establishment of a water power development fund and a fund for the construction of ports and dams and the utilization of water power. These two funds were constituted out of the proceeds of various taxes, including a tax on water power, together with annual subsidies from the State, and loans when necessary. The program of public works drawn up at that time for the following ten years involved a total expenditure of 5,770 million crowns.[98]

Through all these years, during which no action has been taken on Conventions or Recommendations, Czechoslovakia has been in close touch with the I.L.O., as evidenced by the frequent communications from the Government of Czechoslovakia to the International Labor Office, published in Industrial and Labor Information. In November, 1936, the Czechoslovak Minister of Social Welfare, Mr. Necas, was elected Chairman of the Governing Body of the I.L.O. for the ensuing year.[99]

Early in the present year, 1938, the Council of Ministers approved bills for the ratification of the Sheet-glass Workers Convention, 1934, and the Reduction of Hours of Work (Glass Bottle works) Convention, 1935, as well as a bill for the enforcement of the provisions of these Conventions.[100]

---

1 For complete text of the "Memorial of the Czechoslovak Delegation about the Eight Hour Day," see *Official Bulletin*, I, 245.

2 The interest of Czechoslovakia in ratifying Conventions and taking appropriate action to live up to them is shown in the Annual Reports supplied by the Czechoslovak Government and the observations made in some cases on these reports by the Committee of Experts or the Conference Committee on the Application of Conventions. See the following I. L. O. publications:

International Labor Conference Proceedings, 1921-1931.

Record of Proceedings, 1932-1938.

Report of Director, Appendix, 1933-1938.

Summary of Annual Reports under Article 408, 1932-1935 (*under Article 22*, 1936-1938).

Report of Governing Body upon Workings of Conventions, 1931-1938.

3 See *Industrial and Labor Information*, LXVI, Supplement-Chart of Progress of Ratifications, June, 1938, for complete figures.

4 *Summary of Annual Reports Under Article 408*, 1932, p. 5.

5 For the text of the Recommendation concerning unemployment, see *Official Bulletin*, I, 419.

6 For the text of the Act of July 19, 1921, see *Legislative Series*, 1921, Cz. 5. For Summary of the Act and Comparison with the Conventions concerning unemployment, see *supra*, pp. 143-150.

7 Text of Convention concerning unemployment, *Official Bulletin*, I, 417.

8 *Industrial and Labor Information*, L, 308.

9 *Ibid.*, LIX, 385.

10 For the text of the Convention concerning employment of women before and after childbirth, see *Official Bulletin*, I, 422.

11 *Official Bulletin*, II, 21.

12 *Official Bulletin*, IV, 93.

13 For text of the Convention concerning the minimum age for employment of children by night, see *Official Bulletin*, I, 433.

14 *Official Bulletin*, VII, 118.

15 For the text of the Convention concerning the age for admission of children to employment in agriculture, see *Official Bulletin*, IV, 490.

16 For the text of the Convention concerning the application of the weekly rest in industrial undertakings, see *Official Bulletin*, IV, 503.

17 *Handwörterbuch der Staatswissenschaften* (Dritte Auflage; Jena: Verlag von Gustav Fischer, 1909), Erster Band, p. 639.

18 See *Official Bulletin*, IV, 495.

19 *Constitution of the Czechoslovak Republic* (International Conciliation No. 179, 1922).

20 See *Official Bulletin*, IV, 499.

21 *Industrial and Labor Information*, V, 639.

22 *Official Bulletin*, IV, 497.

23 *Twenty-fourth Report of the Commissioner of Labor*, 1909 (Washington: Government Priting Office, 1911), p. 36.

24 The Convention thereby prescribed equality between industrial and agricultural workers in respect of workmen's compensation. Important questions of interpretation have been raised in this connection. See *Report of Governing Body upon Working of Convention concerning Workmen's Compensation in Agriculture, Seventeenth Session*, Geneva, 1933, p. 15.

25 *Official Bulletin*, VIII, 8.

26 For the texts of the Eight Hour Day Act and the Order of Jan. 11, 1919, see *Legislative Series*, 1919, Cz. 1 and Cz. 2.

27 For the text of the Recommendation concerning night work in agriculture, see *Official Bulletin*, IV, 490.

28 For text of the Recommendation, see *Official Bulletin*, IV, 492.

29 *Legislative Series*, 1920, Cz. 2.

30 For the text of the Recommendation concerning the development of technical agricultural education, see *Official Bulletin*, IV, 494.

31 *Industrial and Labor Information*, XXI, 59; XXIII, 400; XXVI, 356.

32 For text of the Recommendation concerning the application of the weekly rest in commercial establishments, see *Official Bulletin*, IV, 506.

33 For the text of the Recommendation concerning social insurance in agriculture, see *Official Bulletin*, IV, 499.

34 See *supra*, p. 66 for compulsory sickness insurance; p. 75 for old-age insurance.

35 For accident insurance legislation, see *supra*, p. 97.

36 For the text of the Recommendation concerning the prevention of unemployment, see *Official Bulletin*, IV, 487.

37 For unemployment insurance legislation, see *supra*, p. 128.

38 For the text of Recommendation concerning the protection before and after childbirth, of women wage-earners in agriculture, see *Official Bulletin*, IV, 489.

39 See *supra*, p. 56.

40 For text of the Recommendation concerning living-in conditions of agricultural workers, see *Official Bulletin*, IV, 494.

41 *Official Bulletin*, X, 174.

42 *Industrial and Labor Information*, XIII, 509.

43 *Ibid.*, XVI, 106.

44 For the text of the Recommendation, see *Official Bulletin*, VIII, 233.

45 *Industrial and Labor Information*, XXI, 19.

46 *Industrial and Labor Information*, XXII, 349.

47 *Industrial and Labor Information*, XXIII, 3.

48 *Industrial and Labor Information*, XXIV, 404.

49 *Official Bulletin*, X, 114, 117.

50 *Report of the Director* (Minutes of the 37th Session of the Governing Body, Berlin: October, 1927), p. 86.

51 More recent figures, taken from Annuaire Statistique de Tchecoslovaquie, 1938, p. 242, are as follows: On December 31, 1936, there were in Czechoslovakia, 699 trade unions with 2,219,100 members including 191 organizations wholly or mainly composed of manual workers with a membership of 1,241,000, and 508 unions of salaried employees and public officials with a membership of 978,000. The largest central trade union organization, the Federation of Czechoslovak Trade Unions, had a membership (including unions of German-speaking workers) of 690,400.—Information received from the I. L. O., Geneva, Switzerland. Similar figures may be found in I. L. O. Year-Book, 1936-1937, pp. 574-575; 586-587.

52 *Industrial and Labor Information*, XXXV, 410.

53 Legislative Series, 1932, Cz. 1.

54 *Industrial and Labor Information*, XLIV, 9.

55 *Ibid.*, XLV, 165.

56 *Official Bulletin*, I, 428.

57 *Industrial and Labor Information*, LIII, 142.

58 *Official Bulletin*, XII, 42.

59 *Industrial and Labor Information*, XXVII, 3.

60 *Legislative Series*, 1920, Int. 3.

61 For summary of the provisions of these treaties, see *supra*, pp. 105-108.

62 *Industrial and Labor Information*, XIII, 550.

63 *Op. cit.*, p. 553.

64 *Industrial and Labor Information*, XVIII, 494.

65 *Industrial and Labor Information*, XXVI, 182.

66 For text of Convention concerning night work in bakeries, see *Official Bulletin*, X, 119.

67 For complete text of both letters, see *Official Bulletin*, XIV, 60-64.

68 *Industrial and Labor Information*, XXXIV, 97.

69 For text of Convention, see *Official Bulletin*, XI, 139.

70 See *supra*, p. 140.

71 *Industrial and Labor Information*, XXVII, 3.

72 For text of Recommendation, see *Official Bulletin*, XI, 143.

73 *Industrial and Labor Information*, XXVIII, 3.

74 *Industrial and Labor Information*, XXVIII, 161.

75 *Ibid.*, XXIX, 97.

76 *Ibid.*, XXXI, 42.

77 *Op. cit.*, XXXI, 134.

78 For legislation regarding holidays with pay, see *supra*, p. 143.

79 *Industrial and Labor Information*, XXIX, 264.

80 For the text of the Recommendation, see *Official Bulletin*, IX, 157.

81 *Industrial and Labor Information*, XXXIII, 405.

82 *Ibid.*, XXIX, 293.

83 For texts of the Convention and Recommendation, see *Official Bulletin*, XIII, 121, 125.

84 For summary of the act of December 12, 1919, see *supra*, p. 36. *Industrial and Labor Information*, XXXI, 333, quotes from the *Bulletin* of the Federation of German Employers in Czechoslovakia to the effect that the ratification of this Convention "would not involve any change in the existing situation in Czechoslovakia" because of this law covering home work and collective agreements in other industries.

85 *Industrial and Labor Information*, XXIX, 323.

86 *Ibid.*, XXXVI, 400.

87 *Ibid.*, XLIX, 66.

88 For the text of the Convention, see *Official Bulletin*, XIV, 921.

89 *Legislative Series*, 1934, Cz. 10.

90 *Industrial and Labor Information*, L, 67.

91 *Official Bulletin*, XV, 60-69.

92 *Industrial and Labor Information*, XL, 195.

93 For text of the Convention relating to hours of work in coal mines, see *Official Bulletin*, XVI, 247.

94 Hours of Work in Coal Mines, Report III, Supplement, International Labor Conference, Fourteenth Session (Geneva, 1930), pp. 94-96.

95 *Industrial and Labor Information*, XLI, 48.

96 *Industrial and Labor Information*, XLI, 48.

97 *Industrial and Labor Information*, XXXVI, 356.

98 *Industrial and Labor Information*, XXXII, 195.

99 *I. L. O. Year*, 1936-37, p. 9.

100 See *supra*, p. 38.

CONCLUSION

THIS account of the labor legislation in Czechoslovakia, with special reference to the standards of the International Labor Organization, is not an exhaustive one. In many respects it is incomplete and unsatisfactory. It does not tell the whole story.

There remain questions, the answers to which could not be found in the materials available, or which would have led beyond the scope of this study. One of these questions is why Czechoslovakia has not ratified certain International Labor Conventions, when to do so would have entailed what appears to be a slight change in existing legislation. Such Conventions are those concerning the employment of women before and after childbirth, the night work of young persons employed in industry, and workmen's compensation for accidents.

In order to understand thoroughly this failure to bring minor points of legislation up to the standards set by International Labor Conventions, it would be necessary to spend some time in Czechoslovakia, studying the current issues of the newspapers and the records of Parliamentary debates, and talking with representatives of employers and workers, as well as government officials.

Another of these questions is whether the progressive labor legislation of Czechoslovakia has been due primarily to the influence of the International Labor Conventions or rather to pressure from their strongly organized labor organizations, or perhaps to the socially-minded character of the Czech people after their release from Hapsburg domination. Here again, the answer could be found only after an intensive study of Czech history and institutions, of the political significance of their trade union organizations, and of the internal economy and its relation to local factors in foreign competition.

Czechoslovakia and Geneva have certainly had important reactions on each other. Much of the labor legislation of

Czechoslovakia existed before the Conventions were adopted. For example, the Act respecting the Eight Hour Day, passed in Czechoslovakia in 1918, provided for the eight hour working day, prohibited the night work of women, provided a weekly rest day in industrial and agricultural undertakings, and fixed a minimum age for admission of children to industrial and agricultural employment before the Conventions concerning these subjects were adopted.

The attitude of the delegates from Czechoslovakia to the International Labor Conference each year has been both sympathetic and helpful. This has been due to the experience of Czechoslovakia in its own legislation which in many cases antedated the discussion of questions at Geneva as a basis of Conventions and Recommendations, and to the pride which the Czechoslovaks have taken in the advanced position of their country in respect of social legislation. Their interest and enthusiasm was contagious at many times in the history of the Conference and certainly operated to encourage reciprocal and cooperative efforts on behalf of social legislation between the I.L.O. and the Czech Government and people.

As a typical illustration of events of this nature, the speech of a Worker's Delegate to the first session of the International Labor Conference, Washington, 1919, Mr. Tayerle, Secretary of the Czechoslovak Federation of Labor in Prague, may be cited. He spoke at some length on the experience of Czechoslovakia under the Eight Hour Day Law which at that time had been in operation for one year.

He described the main features of the law, stating that it permitted a choice between the eight hour day and the forty-eight hour week, and also provided for the measurement of working time by periods of four weeks in such a way that it was possible to apply it to industries of transport and to agriculture, according to the type of the production and the climate.

He went on to say that the Eight Hour Day Law distinguished between overtime necessitated by some catastrophe or accident and that made obligatory by the season or urgent economic reasons; and made provision for so-called preliminary work and continuous work; that is, work in which the change from the day to the night shift and vice versa required a longer day than that corresponding to a forty-eight hour week.

He closed his speech with a recommendation that the draft of the Convention then under discussion be modified so that it would apply to commerce and agriculture as well as to industry. This was not accepted by the Conference, which did, however, include principles similar to those in the Czechoslovak Eight Hour Day Law in respect to industry, in the Hours Convention.[1]

Private communications from Czech sources indicate that the view is commonly held in Czechoslovakia that their experience has made its contribution on other occasions as well as in support of I. L. O. standards.

On the other hand, many Conventions were adopted by the International Labor Conference to ratify which Czechoslovakia had to either pass new laws or amend and supplement existing legislation, much of which was inherited from the Austro-Hungarian Empire. Examples of these are the Conventions concerning the use of white lead in painting, workmen's compensation for occupational diseases, equality of treatment as regards compensation for accidents, and sickness insurance. From the communications sent to the I.L.O. by the Czechoslovak Ministry of Social Welfare, there is no doubt that it was at least partly due to a desire to conform to the standards set up by the International Labor Conventions that Czechoslovakia was so active in passing legislation beneficial to the workers.

The third question not answered satisfactorily is why Czechoslovakia, after having shown so much interest in ratifying Conventions and bringing her legislation up to a high standard, should have slowed down her ratifications since 1929. Only two Conventions have been ratified since then; namely, workmen's compensation for occupational diseases, in 1932, and marking of weight on heavy packages, in 1934. Nothing has been done since then, although the communications from Czechoslovakia to the I.L.O. state that she is still in sympathy with the work of the Organization and has hopes of bringing more of her laws into conformity with its standards.

It is the author's conclusion that this may be explained largely by the economic crisis, which called for the expenditure of huge sums of money for emergency relief work in the way of housing and other public works, leaving little for the extension of the program of labor legislation. It is also clear from the records that the attention of the Government and particularly of the Minister of Social Welfare was taken up to a great extent with the formulating of measures to combat unemployment and bankruptcy. Recently, too, the political development in Central Europe has necessitated the spending of increasingly large amounts of money for national defense. It may be the pall of uncertainty and fear which overhangs the political situation that has taken up the attention of the Government of Czechoslovakia, as well as that of other countries of Europe, to the exclusion of everything else.

The fear of foreign competition, especially that of Germany since she gave up her membership in the I.L.O. and ceased to be bound by the same commitments, has doubtless had its effect on Czechoslovakia. Since 1935, the continuing or recurrent economic depression has not helped the situation in Czechoslovakia in the matter of ratification of draft Conventions.

This is the beginning of a study which the author hopes may some day be enlarged into a social history of Czechoslovakia. In its present state, it serves only to give a glimpse of the framework on which the social life of Czechoslovakia is based. Supplemented and enriched by investigations and study in the country itself and in Geneva, it might be made to show a complete and satisfactory picture of the social life of Czechoslovakia, a new country, which would do justice to the admirable character of the Czech people and their Government.

---

1 *International Labor Conference*, First Annual Meeting, Washington, 1919, p. 54.

BIBLIOGRAPHY

Alden, Percy, Editor, *Hungary of Today*, by Members of the Hungarian Government, London: E. Nash, 1909, 409 p.

Bliss, W. D. F., *What is Done for the Unemployed in European Countries*, Bureau of Labor, Bulletin No. 76, Washington: Government Printing Office, 1908, 277 p.

Brosz, Alex, *Three Years of the Czechoslovak Republic, A Summary of its Progress and Archievements*, Prague: Orbis Printing and Publishing Co., 1921, 40 p.

Bulletins of the International Labor Office, Basle, Vol. I, 1906–Vol. XII, 1917, London: Labor Representation Printing Publishing Co., Ltd.

Caldwell, Robert J., *Economic Situation in Czechoslovakia in 1920*, Washington: Government Printing Office, 1921, 48 p.

Capek, Thomas, Editor, *Bohemia under Hapsburg Misrule; a Study of the Ideals and Aspirations of the Bohemian and Slovak Peoples, as They Relate to and are Affected by the Great European War*, New York, Chicago: Fleming H. Revell Co., 1914, 187 p.

Císař, Jaroslav and Pokorný, F., *The Czechoslovak Republic; A Survey of its History and Geography, its Political and Cultural Organization, and its Economic Resources*, London: Unwin, 1929, 218 p.

Compensation for Industrial Accidents, Studies and Reports, Series M, No. 2, International Labor Office, Geneva, 1925, 655 p.

Constitution of the Czechoslovak Republic, Printed by the "Politika," Prague, 1929, 54 p.

Constitution of the Czechoslovak Republic, The, with introduction by Jiři Hoetzl and V. Joachim. International Conciliation, No. 179, Oct., 1922, Carnegie Endowment for International Peace, New York, 86 p.

Declaration of Independence of the Czechoslovak Nation, by its Provisional Government, Oct. 18, 1918, New York: Marchbanks Press, 8 p.

Gruber, Josef, Editor, *Czechoslovakia; a Survey of Economic and Social Conditions*; New York: Macmillan Co., 1924, 248 p.

Dedek. Dr. Vladimir, "The Constitution of Czechoslovakia," pp. 115-122, *Journal of Comparative Legislation and International Law*, edited for the Society of Comparative Legislation by Sir John Macdonnel and C. E. A. Bedwell, Third Series, Vol. III, London: Society of Comparative Legislation, 1 Elm Court, Temple, E. C. 4, 1921.

Druce, John Gerald Frederick, *In the Heart of Europe, Life in Czechoslovakia*, London: G. Allen and Unwin, Ltd., 1936, 238 p.

Frankel, L. K. and Dawson, M. M., *Workingmen's Insurance in Europe*, New York: Charities Publication Committee, 1910, 477 p.

Gayda, Virginio, *Modern Austria, Her Racial and Social Problems*, London: T. F. Unwin, Ltd., 1915, 350 p.

Gibbon, I. G., *Unemployment Insurance*, London: P. S. King and Son; Orchard House, Westminster, 1911, 354 p.

Graham, Malbone W., *New Government of Central Europe*, London: Sir Isaac Pitman and Sons, Ltd., 1924, 851 p.

Handwörterbuch der Staatswissenschaften

Erste Auflage, herausgegeben von J. Conrad, L. Elster, W. Lexis, Edg. Loening, Jena: Verlag von Gustav Fischer, 1890, Erster Band; "Die Arbeiterschutzgesetsgebung in Oesterreich-Ungarn," pp. 422-433; "Die Arbeiterversicherung in Oesterreich-Ungarn," pp. 530-535.

Zweite Auflage, herausgegeben von J. Conrad, L. Elster, W. Lexis, Edg. Loening, Jena: Verlag von Gustav Fischer, 1898, Erster Band, "Arbeiterschutzgesetzgebung in Oesterreich," pp. 511-521; "in Ungarn," pp. 521-523; "Arbeiterversicherung in Oesterreich-Ungarn," pp. 628-633.

Dritte Auflage, herausgegeben von J. Conrad, L. Elster, W. Lexis, Edg. Loening, Jena: Verlag von Gustav Fischer, 1909, Erster Band "Arbeiterschutzgesetzgebung in Oesterreich-Ungarn," pp. 634-646; "Arbeiterversicherung in Oesterreich-Ungarn," pp. 809-914.

Vierte Auflage, herausgegeben von L. Elster, A. Weber, F. Wieser, Jena: Verlag von Gustav Fischer, 1923, Erster Band; "Die Arbeiterschutzgesetzgebung in Oesterreich," pp. 506-518; "in Ungarn," pp. 570-575; "in der tschechoslowakischen Republic," pp. 602-606; "Solzialversicherung," Siebenter Band, pp. 622-650.

Hours of Labor of Men, Women, and Children Employed In Factories in Austria, U. S. Labor Bureau, Bulletin No. 93, Washington: Government Printing Office, 1911, 25 p.

International Survey of Social Services, 1933, International Labor Office, Geneva, Switz., 1936, Vol. II, 530 p.

Jászi, Oscar, *The Dissolution of the Hapsburg Monarchy*, Chicago: The University of Chicago Press, 1929, 488 p.

Langsam, W. C., *The World Since 1914*, 3rd ed., New York: Macmillan, 1936, 888 p.

McBain, H. L. and Rogers, Lindsay, *New Constitutions of Europe*, New York: Doubleday, Page and Co. (Garden City, 1923), 601 p.

Maurice, C. E., *Bohemia from the Earliest Times to the Foundation of the Czechoslovak Republic in 1918*, London: Unwin, 1922, 376 p.

Mises, L. von, Zur Geschichte der Osterreichischen Fabrikgesetzgebung, in *Zeitschrift für Volkswirtschaft Sozialpolitik und Verwaltung*, XIV, Wien: F. Tempsky, 1905.

Monroe, Will S., *Bohemia and the Czechs, the History, People, Institutions, and Geography of the Kingdom together with accounts of Moravia and Silesia*, Boston: L. C. Page and Co., 1919, 486 p.

Operation of Unemployment Insurance Systems in the U. S. and in Foreign Countries, U. S. Department of Labor, Bureau of Labor Statistics, No. 166, Washington: Government Printing Office, 1934, 121 p.

Pergler, Charles, *The Heart of Europe*, an Address delivered in Washington, Dec. 11, 1916, at a Conference of Oppressed or Dependent Nationalities, Chicago: The Bohemian (Czech) National Alliance, 1917, 39 p.

Pěsek, Josef, *The Story of Czechoslovakia*, translated from the Czech by Marie J. Kohnova, Praha: Professor's Printing House and Library, 1930, 209 p.

Price, George M., *Administration of Labor Laws*, U. S. Department of Labor, Bureau of Labor Statistics, No 142, Washington: Government Printing Office, 1914, 300 p.

Public Old-Age Pensions and Insurance in the U. S. and in Foreign Countries, U. S. Dept. of Labor, Bureau of Labor Statistics, Bulletin No. 561, Washington: Government Printing Office, 367 p.

Publications of the International Labor Office, Geneva, Switzerland:
- Conference Documents
- *Industrial and Labor Information*
- *International Labor Review*
- *Legislative Series*
- *Official Bulletin*
- *Minutes of the Governing Body*
- *Record of Proceedings*, International Labor Conferences
- *Reports of the Director*
- *Summary of Annual Reports under Article 408 (Article 22)*
- Studies and Reports

Rubinow, I. M., *Social Insurance*, New York: Henry Holt and Co., 1933, 525 p.

——, Subsidized Unemployment Insurance and the Ghent System, *Journal of Political Economy*, Vol. XXI, Chicago: University of Chicago Press, 1913.

Senate Document, No. 49, 66th Congress, 1st Session, Senate Documents, Vol. 13, Washington: Government Printing Office, 1919, 184 p.

Seton-Watson, Robert W., *Slovakia Then and Now*, Political Survey by Many Slovak Authors, London: G. Allen and Unwin, Ltd., Prague: Orbis Publishing Co., 1931, 356 p.

Social Policy in the Czechoslovak Republic, edited by the Social Institute of the Czechoslovak Republic for the International Congress on Social Policy in Prague: Orbis Publishing Co., 1924, 246 p.

Temperley, H. W. V., Editor, *A History of the Peace Conference of Paris*, Vol. IV, published under the auspices of Institute of International Affairs, London: Henry Frowde and Hodder and Stoughton, 1921, 528 p.

Treaty of Peace between the Allied and Associated Powers and Austria, together with Other Treaties, Agreements, etc., signed at Saint-Germain-en-Laye, Sept. 10, 1919, London: published by His Majesty's Stationery Office, 1921, 239 p.

Treaties of Peace with Austria and with Hungary and Protocols and Declarations Annexed Thereto, Washington: Government Printing Office, 1920, 249 p.

Unemployment Benefit Plans in the U. S. and Unemployment Insurance in Foreign Countries, Bulletin of U. S. Bureau of Labor Statistics, No. 544, Washington: Government Printing Office, 1931, 385 p.

Veditz, C. W. A., *Child Labor Legislation in Europe*, Bulletin of Bureau of Labor, Department of Commerce and Labor, No. 89, Washington: Government Printing Office, 1910, 436 p.

Workmen's Compensation Legislation of the U. S. and of Foreign Countries, Bulletin of U. S. Department of Labor, Bureau of Labor Statistics, No. 243, Washington, Government Printing Office, 1918, 430 p.; No. 126, 1914, 477 p.

Workmen's Insurance and Compensation Systems in Europe, Twenty-fourth Annual Report, Commissioner of Labor, 1909, Washington: Government Printing Office, 2 Vols., 2749 p.

INDEX

Bei Fragen zur Produktsicherheit wenden Sie sich bitte an:
If you have any questions regarding product safety,
please contact:

Walter de Gruyter GmbH
Genthiner Straße 13
10785 Berlin
productsafety@degruyterbrill.com